MARI...
THANK YOU
FOR SHARING
THE ARE.
SOUL ADVENTURE

2 MAY
97

Life Patterns

Soul Lessons & Forgiveness

by Henry Leo Bolduc

Life Patterns, Soul Lessons, and Forgiveness

First Edition, December 1994
Third Printing, March 1996
Cover illustration by Sue Jones

Library of Congress Catalog Number 94-68926

ISBN Number 0-9601302-4-1

Adventures
Into Time
Publishers
P.O. Box 88 • Independence, VA 24348 • USA

Manufactured in the United States of America
96 95   10 9 8 7 6 5 4 3 2

Contents

Acknowledgments

The information shared in this book is gleaned from more than three decades of my own research. To the best of my knowledge, everything is accurate and authentic; only the names of individuals in the "Case Studies" have been changed to respect their privacy.

Birthing a book is a labor of love — I cannot think of any other reason for doing it. Similar to the birth of a child, there is love, conception, gestation, and — with a few labor pains — the birth itself. With deep appreciation, I thank the following people for giving so generously to the gestation and birthing of this "baby:"

To my wife, Joan Willard Bolduc, whose love of learning is an inspiration to me and to her many students. It takes a lot of love to be a teacher for twenty years. Joan recently received her Master's Degree in Education — she is the love of my life.

To the staff of the Grayson County Public Library, my office away from the office. Priceless wisdom is stored there and it's all FREE!

To chapter editors who helped in the gestation period: Tom Weber, Susan Mayer Bleiberg, Peggy Becker, Jody Menard, Ruby Gillion, Melanie Hertzog, Becky Grey, Roxanne Summers, Egon Frech, Frank Thomas, and Nancy Thomas.

To typists who made sense of my notes: Chris Green, Regina Harris and especially, Virginia Dimmel.

To the gifted artists who made it beautiful: Kathye Mendes, Sue Jones, Jeffrey Winchester, Julia Fierman, Veronica Reed, and Diane Coleman.

A *special thanks* to Baldwin L. Troutman who provided the early help, vision, and encouragement and to Marjorie Reynolds for the final editing. Most of all, Linda Hutchins helped this book at every stage, nurtured it and dedicated herself to its healthy birth.

To all the people who have attended my workshops, classes, and programs. You helped me to fine-tune the work and you gave me great inspiration through your questions and experiences. You inspired this book more than you might realize.

Chapter I

Introduction: *Patterns, Lessons, and Forgiveness*

T he two most important questions you can ask
yourself are:

1. What did I EVER do to deserve THIS?
2. Why am I going through this AGAIN?

When you wonder what you did to deserve THIS,
you are consciously asking your unconscious mind for
insight into the origins of a situation currently being
experienced. Everyone realizes, deep within, that for
every cause there is an effect. For every action there
is a re-action. You wonder what you could have
planted originally in some recent or distant past that
you now reap.

The second question, "Why am I going through
this AGAIN," is even more profound. Here is where you
begin to detect a PATTERN in your life. This pattern
could involve a personal relationship. Perhaps in your
case it is a social, financial, or business matter. What
is important, in order to rectify an uncomfortable situation, is that you recognize that there is, indeed, a
pattern which has been or is being established. That
is the first important step.

Of course, not all patterns are in need of correction. In fact, we all have many positive patterns. Since they don't give us any distress, we tend to overlook them. It is said that great truths can be stated simply and directly. The following is a great truth, somewhat understated. "Positive patterns are fun: challenging patterns are not fun."

What is a pattern? A pattern is a repeating theme or cycle in our lives. It is the mode of behavior, or a combination of actions and qualities, of an individual. A pattern is anything that acts as a model, guide, or stencil from which we form repeated activities. A pattern is interwoven threads that form the fabric of our lives.

Patterns can be either positive and beneficial to us, or they can be difficult and challenging. Positive patterns are like good habits. They make our lives easier, bringing joy and satisfaction. Patterns can be certain skills and special abilities such as attracting abundance and good fortune. For example, many people have a wonderful pattern for loving and nurturing.

On the other hand, challenging patterns are opportunities for growth and learning. They are not "bad," for without challenge we would stagnate and become weak. The challenging patterns can include fears, phobias, and anger. Other negative patterns can be hatred, prejudice, elitist activities, and ego drives.

This book can assist you in the process of discovering your own patterns. It may ask some important questions, but you alone can answer them candidly and honestly. As you read further, you will find new ways to approach your study of self with practical tools like journal writing and defining ideals. Together we will look into such spiritual methods as self-hypnosis, meditation, and past-life evaluation. You may ask what past lives have to do with your current patterns and everyday responses. The research of decades has uncovered the fact that the "roots" of our actions go far deeper than yesterday, last year, or even a long ago childhood.

Chapter II

The Patterns of Your Lives

A. Exploring the Inner Mind

The history of every soul (the cumulative total of the experiences of many lifetimes, spanning thousands of years) is recorded in the subconscious mind. Most of us do not have conscious memory of those experiences. Even though we may not realize it, such unconscious recall can have a direct and profound effect upon our actions and decisions in this lifetime. If we could gain access to the record of our past, it truly would be the adventure of our lives.

If you are skeptical of past-life experience, just for a few minutes suspend your disbelief, open your mind, and boldly enter through a new door and into a new realm. Embark upon a journey of exploration – of adventure and discovery. You will be exploring the mysteries of your inner self, where the soul's history is recorded.

The science of exploring the mysteries of the human soul – the part of us that is *most* human – is called "mysticism," and the explorers who study it are known as regressionists. Their work is analogous to that of archaeologists, who study sites and artifacts of historic or prehistoric peoples. Regressionists, the ar-

chaeologists of the soul, dig through the strata and
sub-strata of memory rather than through the records
of geology. They sift through the potsherds of a broken past, discovering what may be of value and what
may be discarded as unimportant or even harmful.
They reassemble mosaics for a clearer view of the
ancient ways of past lives.

Those explorers of the inner mind discover the
hidden dimensions of the past and display them for
present evaluation. They are the guides who can lead
you on your journey. While the primary research of the
regressionist is the study of the past, regressionists
are also pioneers on the frontiers of tomorrow. They
are progressionists and map-makers of undiscovered
realms and future dimensions of reality.

B. Implications of Past Lives

The mysteries of the human mind have been a
"dark continent" for centuries. It is not a final frontier,
however, but a vast new world – an *explorium!* Mind
is the pathway through time, from past to present to
future. The mind is vast, and contains an amazing
paradox: every living person *has* a mind; yet, most
people are afraid of its potential. Perhaps they are
more concerned with their darker sides – those parts
of themselves they would rather not face.

Everyone has had faults and contradictions
throughout many lives and experiences. Like the earth
herself, each soul has numerous fault lines hidden
beneath the surface. The soul also has sensitive "vol-
canic" hot-spots which can erupt at times of stress,
and with explosive fury; nonetheless, people develop

more quickly and gain more wisdom through being challenged, rather than through being pampered. When people realize that hard lessons are for their growth and betterment, they become wiser.

The experiences and lessons from past lives always influence (and often deeply) one's present life, sometimes in unusual and unexpected ways. In truth, we have experienced all aspects of life everywhere. This revelation is so profound that many would prefer to dismiss the entire concept rather than to explore their memories. We have experienced life in both genders; we have lived lives among various races and adhered to diverse religions. We have inhabited numerous lands and taken citizenship in many nations.

As a result of our varied experiences, we have learned lessons, hopefully, from those past times and places. With this learning comes the recognition and assurance of our common bond or link with ALL humanity. The goal of each life is to grow spiritually in such a way as to strengthen this common bond. In this manner, all souls are strengthened and all lives on the physical plane are enriched.

The subconscious memories of our past lives can have both positive and negative influences on our current life. For example, oftentimes, a person who was oppressed in a past life comes back to become an oppressor in the present life. An even more wicked form of dysfunction can develop – the victim role. In this case a person returns again and again in a futile pattern of re-runs.

Let us consider the plight of the American Indians who were persecuted and robbed in their past; yet, many return to re-enact similar lives. If we have once lived as an American Indian, for instance, how can we deny the plight of today's Indians? Is not that very soul memory (though deep within) a living force today?

WHAT THEME OR PATTERN CAN YOU DETECT?
Artist: Kathye Mendes

C. Learning From Our Past

Our past-life memories are hidden, and yet, if we want to benefit from the experiences of our past, how can we do it? This book contains scripts for "Inner

Adventures," to help you journey safely into your memories. This journey is called "past-life regression." With proper use, it is a powerful TOOL to sever the chains of the past. Sometimes the chains are visible, and sometimes invisible. When the chains are broken, you can develop your present humanity and proceed to build your best possible future.

Before starting on this journey, you need to ask yourself what it is that you are seeking. What questions should you be asking? How can you benefit best from the answers? On a personal level, the question is not WHO you were in a past life, but how you gained spiritually. How did you gain, or how did you lose? How well and how kindly did you play the Game of Life? Did you work to improve yourself, your family, your community?

Regression work is the process, not the product. HOW you learned and how you used that learning is far more important than WHO you were or WHERE you lived. What you were INSIDE is much more valuable than what you appeared to be on the outside.

Let's consider an analogy. Suppose you dress in a costume for a Halloween party. Do you become the person or thing that you are dressed as? Of course not! The outer garb is to create an illusion – the inner person remains the real you. Thus, your outward appearance in a past life is of minor importance. WHAT you were, spiritually and the lessons you learned, are what is of value. The soul's memory is your true wisdom.

D. Why We Have More Than One Life

I believe that, for more than any other reason, we have been granted more than one lifetime to learn lessons. One important lesson is that of FORGIVE-NESS. Most people say that they forgive others, but the reality is that few of us really do so. People say one thing, but often *do* quite the contrary. The many experiences and lessons learned in other lifetimes enable us to forgive much more easily.

Let's suppose, for instance, that a person has stolen something (and we probably have all done a certain amount of stealing in our many lives). In the present life, others – almost always – will think of that person as a thief, even though the individual might possess numerous other excellent qualities. People who have stolen, for whatever reason (perhaps in desperation to keep their families fed) are labeled thieves, and the label sticks.

Thank God we are given a break from all that and can have a new and clean start. That new start is a new life! We are given another chance to learn and to grow toward our goal of spiritual betterment.

Your personal regression history is a significant chapter in the history of humanity. Each life contains pages of splendor and pages of travail, times of wonder and growth, and episodes of loss. Such experiences are what life is all about! Regression exercises are like gifts that refresh your inner memory. They are like pieces of a complex puzzle that you carefully and patiently fit together to see the full picture.

Earlier I stated that regressionists are also progressionists. Regressions help you to review your past and to strengthen your present. Progressions help you to plan for your future. You must *conceive* a wiser, happier, and healthier future before you can start building it. Everywhere, there are cynics and critics who will try to deny you the right to change and to grow. Don't let them stop you! Use soul exploration to connect you with your own heritage. Define your present life ideals and patterns. This will help you to clear a pathway to your *best possible future.*

Chapter III
Working With Difficult Patterns

A. Identifying Negative Patterns: Denial, Re-run, Extremes

There are two basic ways of working with challenging patterns. First, there is the reactionary or defensive approach which includes denial, re-run over and over, or opposite extremes; secondly, there is a positive approach.

Denial

Oh, how easy it is for us all simply to deny any involvement. This approach is very popular in the current age. We find this principle even at the very highest levels of government, i.e. a past-president who "forgot" involvement in illegal deals with enemy governments.

Instead of blaming our leaders, let us identify that same denial in ourselves. Let us be observant of our own "excuses." Let us listen to our own words, making sure our actions are congruent with our inner selves. (This is not always easy to do.)

When we realize that we are involved in negative patterns, the first step is to identify the patterns. It is easier if we choose someone else as an example, so let us look at a young man in our neighborhood. He is an average teenager, interested in sports, music, and friends. Since he got his driver's license a year ago, he has been involved in four accidents.

He hit a dog at the time of the first accident, saying, "The dog ran in front of me, it was his fault."

In the second accident he hit an elderly lady's car, as she was making a turn. At that time he offered, "She was turning too slowly; it was her fault."

The third time, when he drove into a ditch, he said, "It was the road's fault."

In the fourth accident he went off an embankment. While two wreckers pulled out the vehicle, he insisted, "It was the weather's fault."

Do you get the idea? Although there may be some truth in the explanation of each accident, the larger truth is called "projection," a form of "denial." The neighbors have commented on the young man's fast driving habit. The real problem, or the pattern here, is the speed. The accidents are only a symptom of going at an excessive speed. He refuses to take responsibility and blames the problem on others or on circumstances. By living in denial he cannot change, for he has not perceived the pattern or the causal problem. Other expressions of denial can include repression, blame, anger, confrontation, etc.

Re-Run

Re-run is another interesting approach to patterns! The faces may change, the addresses may change, the dates may change, but the basic situation is the same. A classic example of this pattern is a person born into a family which is experiencing alcoholism, and who then becomes an alcoholic and/or marries one. Fortunately, AA and other 12-Step Programs have been of immense help with this pattern in recent years.

Often, this kind of pattern is associated with a "rut," or habit, that gets deeper and more entrenched with the passage of time. When working with most relationship patterns, the re-run approach is most often used.

Extremes

However strange it may sound, we all have learned that, in the fields of electricity and magnetism, it is the OPPOSITES that attract. The same principle applies to humans as well. Perhaps you already know, for example, an alcoholic who gets sober and then becomes a tireless speaker for sobriety. We all have known ex-cigarette smokers who have become crusaders for clean air. Church revival meetings almost always include a street-gang member who has made a 180 degree turn-around to condemn street violence.

As laudable as their goals may be, there is one thing of importance to consider. Are not the two extremes just two examples of the same pattern? Two sides of the same coin? Don't re-act to events from either extreme position. Find a middle ground of balance and moderation.

Going to an opposite extreme gives the illusion, but not the reality, of healing. It is only a form of distancing from the problem or pattern, and merely proceeding to a different one. No matter how it appears, it IS the opposite side of the coin of the SAME BASIC PROBLEM.

B. A Positive Approach

1. Analyze the situation to discover the pattern(s)
2. Research and study ways to heal the pattern
3. Surrender to a higher power
4. Work with trusted friends or support groups
     There are many tools you can use in your work. Among those proven successful are: prayer, meditation, self-hypnosis, self-discipline, journal writing, and going on a personal retreat.

     Some patterns are so obvious that it is hard to miss them. Others are so subtle that it takes careful observation to perceive them. Trusted friends and support groups can be helpful because they can assist us in identifying patterns we can't see ourselves. Later in this book, you will find a number of worksheets that will help greatly in the study of your own patterns.

     The POSITIVE patterns are fun and enjoyable. They make life easier. By identifying them we can develop and utilize them more fully. Again, trusted friends and support groups can help us to clearly see our own strengths and gifts. Positive approaches can also include humor, detachment, or any form of therapy a person might choose.

     Whether positive or challenging, the "roots" of our patterns go deeper than our current lifetime. Our origins are deeper and our purposes greater than most people realize.

Chapter IV

Discovering Your Inner Self

(Tools and Techniques for Understanding Your Patterns and Lessons)

Understanding comes with study, contemplation, and seclusion. I am going to offer you three proven methods of studying and evaluating your inner self, as a means of gaining a deeper understanding of your larger self. Choose the method that feels most comfortable to you. This is the way to obtain the best results. Examine the ideas that I will present and choose one, or any combination of them, or create your own innovative approach. The most important thing is actually to *use* a method of discovering your inner self. This is the way to understand both yourself and your patterns.

A. Journal Writing

This is a fun, free, and enlightening method. All that you need is to set aside 15 – 20 minutes a day, and to bring a pen, and paper. To get the most out of journal writing, put your expectations aside and have fun with it. You will find that you will laugh, grasp at an illusive memory, and so piece together your patterns. Journal writing leads to active learning about yourself, your world, other people, and life.

Keeping a journal can be a journey to self-discovery and a potent morale booster, especially if one writes about one's feelings and emotions. It can be one of the most important tools for building a happier, more productive life, as it helps to open doors that might have remained closed — doors to the deeper inner self as well as doors to the outer, every-day world.

One of the nice things about journal writing is that there is almost no cost involved, except that of pen and paper. If you like, you may purchase a spiral-bound notebook, or a 3-ring binder, which will make it easier to categorize your subject material. Another nice aspect of keeping a journal is that you don't have to undergo any special training, take any classes, or do any other preparation. You can start right now — TODAY! You simply begin right where you are in life by putting your thoughts and feelings on paper. It's that easy.

Many people associate journal writing with keeping a diary. A diary is certainly one form of journal, but it is not the only one. Other types are autobiographical writing, intuitive writing, dream records, writing of future goals and ambitions, and even letter and story writing.

Keeping a journal:
*   Helps you to discover goals, ideals, hopes, fears – just about everything there is about you.
*   Teaches you to **listen** better — and listening more acutely inspires better writing.
*   Teaches you to **observe** better — and observation

brings vision to your writings.

* Teaches you to touch life more deeply — and this depth brings more feeling into your writings.

* Helps with self-honesty, personal integrity, and clarifies thinking.

* Is a safe outlet for hurt, rejection, or reaction. It is you communicating with the **real** you.

* Substantiates your thoughts and experiences. Later you can reflect on them and gain different perspectives over time.

* Gives a feeling of accomplishment. Like exercising your physical body, writing exercises your mind.

* Opens a door to self-discovery by accessing your subconscious mind. Past-life insights are often revealed in writing.

Your best writing often comes through the most difficult times — from the most challenging lessons and experiences.

Patterns will begin to show throughout your life as you study your journal. Those patterns are vital to your learning and growth — they are the real *lessons* in your life.

Use all of your senses as you write. Use words descriptive of what you: **SEE, HEAR, TOUCH, SMELL, TASTE.** Also, be aware of the 6th sense that you will discover inside. This is your **INNER RE-SPONSE.**

Parents, give your children a diary (with a lock) and encourage them to write in it, so that they can discover, early in life, the immense value of such creative writing. They will learn the healing power of expressing themselves through sincere expression of their thoughts.

If your language is imperfect or limited, learn to use a thesaurus. To improve your grammar, there are many books that could help. One favorite is a slim volume entitled **THE ELEMENTS of STYLE,** by Strunk and White, published by the McMillan Company. For a spelling problem, get a dictionary or use the spell check that comes with most word processors. If you plan to do any professional writing, use of a word processor will make editing your documents much easier and will increase your productivity.

Keeping a journal helps you to write better, to think more clearly, to assimilate the experiences of your life. In time you may return to your writing and re-live those great experiences and more wisely re-evaluate the challenging times. Reading something you wrote in the past gives insight as to how your life has changed — progressed. This is part of your personal history which, most likely, is lost if it is not recorded. Reflecting upon the past helps to facilitate personal growth.

Finally, as emphasized earlier, don't procrastinate. Go ahead and start your journal writing now. You will find it an enriching experience. Use the power of the pen to get a better understanding of your lessons and patterns – and yourself!

Here are some suggested "story starters" to motivate you and get you going:

"I behave just like my Mom when I ....."

"A recurring dream I've had is ....."

"The quality I admire most in others is ....."

"The thing that irritates me most in other people is ....."

"I find myself attracting the same kind of man/
woman ....."
"If I have had a past life, I would have lived in ....."
"I would have worked in that life as ....."
"My forefathers came to this country from ....."

After you've written your story, let your family or
friends critique it. You'll learn how to discipline your
thoughts, how to use correct grammar, how to research material, and many other useful techniques.
Furthermore, you will give pleasure or impart knowledge to those who read your story. You may even get
a story published. Then you can call yourself an author!

Your journal is the **"BOOK OF YOUR LIFE,"** a
document of the **real** you. It is for you and you alone,
unless you wish to share all or part of it with others.

1. Keeping a Diary

In its most basic form, a diary is simply a day-by-
day account of the events in your life that you would
like to record for future reference. Many people in the
business world or in public life keep such records to
refresh their memories of past events or commitments
they may have made. They often include in the diary
a calendar of future engagements and so forth. The
diary, or daily journal, thus becomes an important
reference in their daily activities. In their private lives,
people who keep journals often include such entries
in their autobiographical journals.

2. Autobiographical Writing

Autobiographical writing can be for you alone (unless you wish to share it with very special friends). Knowing that it is for your eyes only, you can feel more comfortable in expressing your innermost feelings and emotions. In times of stress and trouble, keeping this journal can be very therapeutic. The simple act of putting your thoughts on paper can give you a new perspective to your problems. Studies conducted by James Pennebaker, Ph.D., Professor of psychology at Southern Methodist University in Dallas, have demonstrated the benefits of writing about traumatic experiences.

Dr. Pennebaker asked students to write for 15 minutes a day, choosing as their subject either a traumatic experience or a superficial topic. "We found those people who write about thoughts and feelings typically show significant improvements in physical health and improved function, have fewer doctor visits, and report feeling happier and healthier in the months that followed," says Pennebaker.

Although the initial effect of the writing sessions might be to make the person sadder, a positive outlook and lighter mood resulted within two to three weeks, and persisted for as long as six months afterward. So, although you may feel sad or depressed immediately after writing, within a day or two you should begin to feel a sense of relief and contentment. In writing about such experiences, describe the event and your deepest emotions, but do not rationalize or lay blame. Just try to understand your thoughts.

In addition to writing about difficult experiences,

LET YOUR HEART DO THE WRITING
Artist: Jeffrey Winchester

you may also write about your accomplishments, your successes, your joys, and your hopes – all to your benefit. When you write about any of your thoughts and experiences, you automatically assimilate them, learn, and grow wiser. This prepares you to face similar situations in the future. So, let's get started on this wonderful discovery of self. To make the initial effort easy, let's begin with a small project. Later you will want to begin your permanent record, or your autobiographical journal — this can be its beginning.

Write a few paragraphs about:

1. Childhood experiences
   a. Positive or pleasant
   b. Negative or unpleasant

2. Present-day experiences
   a. Family
   b. Work
   c. Travel
   d. Pets
   e. Hobbies
   f. An influential person in your life

3. Future Plans
   a. Hopes
   b. Fears
   c. Work
   d. Personal plans

3. Intuitive Writing

If you encounter difficulty in writing about your hopes, plans, emotions, and feelings, try writing from a different level – adopt a new style. What I'm describing here is not a type of journal, but a writing style which can be used in any of the journal types. This writing style is called free-form, or free-flow. It has no rules except just to write — let the writing go where it wishes. Get out of your own way and just **DO IT!** Let's examine the techniques of this writing style:

1. Stream of consciousness technique
   You simply begin by writing down everything that comes into your mind, regardless of whether it makes any sense.

2. Ideals
   First, sit quietly and reflect upon a problem that is currently affecting your life. Next, ask your inner mind, or your higher mind, for a solution to that problem. When you receive the answer, write down the solution in your journal. For example, experiment with this technique to connect with your higher self to ask the following questions:
   a. What do you *really* want to do with your life, and why?
   b. How would you act even if you were certain you'd never be found out or blamed?
   c. How would you act even if you were certain you'd never receive any recognition or credit?

3. Poetry and prose
   Often the language of the subconscious, or the inner mind, comes through in either rhyme or blank verse. If it does, work with those tools in your intuitive writing. Work with whatever tools your subconscious advises. Just follow the guidance of your intuition. Those who are musically inclined may wish to write songs.

4. Dreams

Most self-help, spiritual, and psychological materials will advise you to keep a dream journal. They also advise you to encourage dreaming by telling yourself that you will remember your dreams upon awakening. If you have an unresolved problem from the day's activities, relate the problem to your subconscious mind and ask it to give you a solution in a dream. Tell yourself to awaken after each dream so that you can record it before it is lost. The dream journal can be kept separate from, or included within, your writing journal.

Dreams are an important part of your communication with your inner mind. Your dreams are messages to you from your subconscious; they are intended to give you guidance from your higher self. Unfortunately, most people do not recognize that their dreams contain guidance, and they forget them immediately upon awakening. Your conscious mind, which is controlled by your ego, or personality, does not recognize dreams for what they are. When you awaken, you most likely will be conscious of your last dream, and think that you will remember it. But if you stir around, or get out of bed, your conscious mind may take over and the dream will be gone.

In view of the unique manner in which dreams are received, if you are to benefit from them, you must record them immediately upon awakening, or they, most likely, will be lost. Thus, you could keep a separate dream journal by your bedside, where you could make entries before your conscious mind becomes alert enough to erase them. This can be done by keeping a notebook and pencil by your bed and recording the dreams before you engage your conscious mind. If you sleep alone, or have a tolerant partner, you can record them into a cassette recorder. If you tell yourself to wake up after each dream, you may be able to record several dreams in a single night.

You will soon observe that your subconscious speaks to you in symbols, some symbols are universal, some are personal. You will have to learn to interpret those symbols, and you will be able to do so with practice. Go back through your dream journal from time to time and you may be able to identify trends, patterns, or other signs by which you can learn to use the messages your dreams are sending you, for surely they are messages from your subconscious.

5. Letter-Writing

Most people would not associate letter writing with keeping a journal; however, it is much akin to it. In fact, many famous people in the past published such correspondence. Thus you may think of your correspondence as a type of journal writing. If you kept copies of your correspondence, you would soon realize that it was actually a part of your autobiographical journal. If you like, you can use parts of your autobiographical journal in your letters.

Sometimes letter writing can be therapeutic. By way of illustration, let me give you an example taken from the experience of a friend. "Once, many years ago, I became incensed with what I perceived to be lack of proper recognition for certain work I had performed, and wrote an angry letter to the individual concerned. Before mailing the letter, I showed it to a colleague for whom I had great respect. He said, 'Okay, you've written a good letter, and got the matter off your chest. Now throw it in the trash basket.' I thought about it and agreed with him. The act of writing the letter had, indeed, released the matter from my system, and I felt better about it. Many times since then, I have remembered that advice and followed it." The next time that you need to release some tension, try writing a letter about it and then throw the letter away.

As with any other activity, one learns and gains experience and wisdom with practice. So let's begin by writing three letters to friends, loved ones, someone in a nursing home — **anyone** you know. Your letters will be appreciated and you will gain from it. But this time, put stamps on them and mail them! Even more challenging, but very productive, is to write "letters to the editor" of any state-wide or national publication concerning topics of current interest or of particular concern to you. You may be surprised at the response.

6. Story-Writing

I can hear some of you say, "**Story writing!!** I'm not an author. I can't write a story." In fact, statistics reveal that 90% of Americans think that they cannot write creatively. Well, you'll never know unless you try. First, don't think about writing an entire book; think in more modest terms. Write about something familiar – a few pages about your family, or your family history. Write as though you were talking to a friend; just let the story tell itself. So don't procrastinate; sit down and **do it!!**

B. A Spiritual Sanctuary

Create a Spiritual Sanctuary. Find or make a special place in your home or on your land where you can go for contemplation. This place does not have to be of a certain structure — just a secluded nook, or area. Bring your favorite momentos and most cherished objects.

Learning is a life-long experience. We are in this Earth School to learn and to grow, not only during our adolescent years, but throughout our entire lives. Our goals can be to grow, to develop, to improve, to accomplish, to have adventures, and just to be kind! Learning can improve with age.

Distractions in daily life make continued learning difficult. The creation of a spiritual sanctuary will set up the environment for your continued growth. This will be your personal space — a place where you can go for quiet, for contemplation, and for rest. There are many ways to create your space. For example, use a library, take over a large closet in your home, use the corner of a room, or find a secluded place on your property that might work for you.

If you are having a problem creating a space for yourself because your home environment is so cluttered that you can't clear out a little area for your spiritual sanctuary, something is definitely wrong! Make your spiritual goals *primary*, not secondary. Learn to be still, to be sincere, to simplify your daily life, and to magnify your spiritual life. Grasp the **REAL MEANING** of your life and live it exuberantly.

Our spiritual sanctuaries are there for our growth. They provide a place for rest. This rest is vital for growth and learning. Following periods of great activity, we often need quiet time to evaluate and to understand what we have just experienced. This quiet time often provides us with more than just understanding. It is often a time of inspiration and the incubation of new plans and strategies.

If music is an important part of your life, be sure to include it in your plans. If your sanctuary is out of doors, bring chimes, drums, or a portable cassette player.

A spiritual sanctuary is your own wonderful, peaceful, and private place to explore your thoughts, your feelings, your innermost heart. This is your peaceful place to pray and to meditate.

Have fun creating your own personal, restful, healing place. It is easy to build anywhere, indoors or out. Just make the focal point your favorite items, your momentos — *anything* from your life that has meaning. Decorate your space with elegance or simplicity; it's up to you. Create beauty — bring hope and har-

SPIRITUAL SANCTUARY
Artist: Jeffrey Winchester

mony, and enjoy the doing. Start with a candle or two
if you wish, a gift from a friend or a loved one, a beautiful piece from nature herself — some special rock or
mineral, a feather or a sea shell, souvenirs from enchanted journeys or vacations. Sacraments are any
objects that are sacred to *you*. Bring them to your
sanctuary.

Now begin to add the personal, human element.
Perhaps a small mirror so that you can look deeply
into the eyes of your own soul. Add to this a photo if
you wish, a picture of a favorite saint or other holy
person — anyone whom you hold as an ideal. Bring
anything which reminds you of your real essence, of
the **real** you, that unique, wonderful, precious **you**. A
you that is kind, generous, and loving, the you that
you truly wish to express with an attitude of reverence
in the fullness of your heart and soul. Continue adding new items from time to time as your life grows,
progresses, and evolves. Acknowledge and appreciate
each adventure in this great school or learning center
that we call the Earth School.

Your sacred place — your Altar — is for you to
enjoy. It is good to come here. Come at regular times
simply to commune, to relax, just to be **you**. Is it only
your imagination that this place — this sanctuary —
has made a difference in your life? Even if it is only
imagination, there is wisdom in accepting that there
may be more to life than some would openly admit.

This is the place to contemplate your spiritual
friends, your loved ones, your guardian angel, your
protectors, those that may not be visible to the outer
eyes but may be seen by the inner eyes. Do the inner
eyes see more clearly? Do the inner ears hear more

acutely? Does the inner heart feel more deeply? Your friends in the Spirit Lands may wish to come and visit you in your sacred sanctuary. If you will it, they will come.

"IF YOU BUILD IT, THEY WILL COME"
Artist: Kathye Mendes

It is always good to connect with loved ones from the past and even into future time. Just build your sanctuary! Just do it! They will come.

Bring your journal to your spiritual sanctuary so

that you may record your heart's memories and your soul's visions in your peaceful, quiet space. (Your spiritual sanctuary may become the place where you always engage in journaling).

Important things to remember are: practice silence — don't talk about it; do it. Be joyous — being spiritual does not mean being somber, morose, or withdrawn. It *does* mean to live your life fully and thankfully.

We have examined journal writing and the spiritual sanctuary and we can see how the two of them could act separately or together to work for your growth and learning. Let's look at a third way, a personal retreat.

C. Take a Learning Vacation: A Personal Retreat

Take time out for a personal retreat away from your daily routine. I like to describe this as a spiritual adventure. Others call it a "weekend get-away." It is a meditative "outward bound" for the "inward bound." The rewards may be life-changing. The cost involved may be as small or as large as you choose to make it.

About thirty years ago, after graduating from high school, I contemplated what my life's direction and vocation might be. Although I had a good job working at an apple orchard, I knew that it would never be my career.

I decided to take a few days out of my busy schedule to go on a personal retreat. A friend in New Hampshire owned a small mountain lake completely surrounded by woods – a winding trail was the only access. It sounded like the perfect place to go.

Because I did not own a tent, I brought a tarp to construct a temporary "lean-to" shelter. I carried in my sleeping bag, books, paper, and toilet paper. I brought no food because I had read that the American Indians fasted when they went on their "vision quest."

Originally, I planned a four-day weekend retreat. The first two days passed slowly — too slowly. I read, built a campfire and seriously wondered why I had decided to do such a "boring" thing. I probably would have given-up and returned home, except that I had told people about my adventure and I didn't want them to think that I had "chickened-out."

The next two days were more productive. As I meditated, used self-hypnosis and prayed for guidance, I began to list what I wanted to do with my life. Then I wrote what I did NOT want to do. Slowly the realization came that, with work and dedication, I could do just about anything! So what did I **really** want to do? What interested and excited me the most in life?

In the process of writing the things I most wanted to do, the answer became obvious. For a couple of years, I had been conducting experiments in past-life exploration, after reading *The Search for Bridey Murphy*, by Morey Bernstein. This was very exciting work, but what could I do, realistically, with such information?

Then I remembered reading about Edgar Cayce, from Virginia Beach, Virginia, who spoke about past lives. Slowly, a thought started to form, "Why not go to Virginia Beach to learn more?" Although Mr. Cayce had died the year before I was born, I knew that an

**SAMPLING SERENITY — AN ADVENTURE
INTO THE HEART OF NATURE**

Artist: Jeffrey Winchester

organization of people was carrying on his work.

A thought was born, a spark was ignited in the chasm of my brain! An inner prompting, a plan or action was formulated on the shore of that secluded New Hampshire lake. This was not some blinding vision nor did trumpets sound in the sky, but a real direction was now evident: "Travel! Go to that Cayce place."

Perhaps the thought and the plan would have come to me in spite of taking a retreat. Perhaps a few days of fasting were unnecessary – who knows? But I *did* gain something. I made a decision to take a new road – and certainly one less traveled!

Within a few months I was on my way to Virginia Beach to become a member of the Association for Research and Enlightenment. Now, three decades later, I journey the same pathway. I continue to reach out through presenting workshops and educational programs around the world for the A.R.E. OUTREACH is my mission!

You also can take a personal retreat — your own inner quest. Plan *your* spiritual adventure now. It does not have to be a trip to the woods. Do what is comfortable for you, yet will allow you the opportunity to explore your inner self and to receive any messages that you may be given. Whatever kind of retreat it is, should it make you more comfortable and more willing to take the spiritual adventure, do it. You might choose a safe motel that is secluded, with no distractions, or go to a cabin in the woods, or to a hotel on a secluded beach, or to the house of a friend who is away for a few days. Your expenses may be increased but the important thing is that you go away and explore your inner being.

Perhaps your experience will be as mine; perhaps not. Nonetheless, your spiritual retreat can bring you various benefits. You can:

* Connect with your innermost self.
* Be given valuable guidance – a dream, a vision or a plan of action.
* Enjoy the beauty and splendor of nature.
* Receive insight into what is REALLY important in your life.
* Experience solitude, rest, and quiet reflection.

Best of all your spiritual adventure can cost very little, yet give you high-yield returns. You could choose to do as I did, keeping things simple and easy. Choose a safe, secluded site (*not* during hunting season)! Bring what you already have, or borrow from friends:

- a tent or tarp
- sleeping bag
- pen, paper, toilet paper
- knife, matches, drinking water

Leave the electronic gadgets at home. This is a *spiritual* adventure, an inner quest.

Although most people are aware of the importance of building their minds and bodies, few are aware of the greater importance of building their spirits. Though often neglected, spirit is the life essence — the vital living force.

Eventually, each person must stop and re-evaluate life. Sometimes a tragedy triggers such a situation. It is better not to wait for circumstances to propel us onto a higher path. Specifically choose a spiritual adventure or exercise. When that is accomplished a larger view is presented, an inner guidance is heard, a deeper purpose is realized. Such profound revelations guide us to our spiritual destiny. Pivotal or transformative events can bring positive change and betterment.

In the time of the American Indian, a "vision quest" was practiced by the young men. Sadly, there is little recorded history of the importance of spiritual exercises and quests for the young women. It is even more ironic that, today, women are more interested in building their spiritual lives than are men. Perhaps this is a natural balance, or perhaps women have grown wiser while men have become more distracted. In any case, women can now take the great journey — the holy quest — as equally as men. Perhaps they will be even more dedicated in purpose, richer in ideals, braver in discovery. **EVERYONE** has the God-given right to become a spiritual seeker, and to experience the adventure!

After my own youthful quest, another decade passed before I located a book that gave practical information about how the American Indian approached his spiritual retreat. That book, *THE SOUL of the INDIAN*, by Charles Alexander Eastman (Ohiyesa), was first published in 1911 "to paint the religious life of the typical American Indian as it was before he knew the white man." In 1980 the University of Nebraska Press reprinted that small but immensely valuable book.

Eastman wrote powerfully yet poetically:
"The worship of the 'Great Mystery' was silent, solitary, free from all self-seeking. It was silent, because all speech is of necessity feeble and imperfect; therefore the souls of my ancestors

ascended to God in wordless adoration. It was solitary, because they believed that He is nearer to us in solitude, and there were no priests authorized to come between a man and his Maker.

"There were no temples or shrines among us save those of nature. Being a natural man, the Indian was intensely poetical. He would deem it sacrilege to build a house for Him who may be met face to face in the mysterious, shadowy aisles of the primeval forest, or on the sunlit bosom of virgin prairies, upon dizzy spires and pinnacles of naked rock, and yonder in the jeweled vault of the night sky! He who enrobes Himself in filmy veils of cloud, there on the rim of the visible world where our Great-Grandfather Sun kindles his evening campfire, He who rides upon the rigorous wind to the north, or breathes forth His spirit upon aromatic southern airs, whose war-canoe is launched upon majestic rivers and inland seas — He needs no lesser cathedral!

"That solitary communion with the Unseen which was the highest expression of our religious life is partly described in the word *bambeday*, literally "mysterious feeling," which has been variously translated "fasting" and "dreaming." It may better be interpreted as "consciousness of the divine."

"The first *bambeday*, or religious retreat, marked an epoch in the life of the youth, which may be compared to that of confirmation or conversion in Christian experience. Having first prepared himself by means of the purifying vapor-bath, and cast off as far as possible all human or fleshly influences, the young man sought out the noblest height, the most commanding summit in all the surrounding region. Knowing that God sets no value upon material things, he took with him no offerings or sacrifices other than symbolic objects, such as paints and tobacco. Wishing to appear before Him in all humility, he wore no clothing save his moccasins and breech-cloth. At the solemn hour of sunrise or sunset he took up his position, overlooking the glories of the earth and facing the "Great Mystery," and there he remained, naked, erect, silent, and motionless, exposed to the elements and forces of His arming, for a night and a day to two days and nights, but rarely longer. Sometimes he would chant a hymn without words, or offer the ceremonial "filled pipe." In this holy trance or ecstasy the Indian mystic found his highest happiness and the motive power of his existence."

Eastman continues to explain that when the individual returned to camp, he (or she), must again enter the vapor-bath (sweat lodge). The sign or vision given to the seeker was usually kept private or personal, unless instructed otherwise. Occasionally, at the end of his life, a man may discuss his original vision-quest. Eastman wrote, "Sometimes an old man, standing upon the brink of eternity, might reveal to a chosen few the oracle of his long-past youth."

Obviously, I didn't wait as long to reveal to you my "vision," or decision to travel. Nonetheless, the passage of time has proven my original guidance to be both wise and productive.

Of the three methods presented for gaining guidance to the inner self, any or all of them may be compatible with your needs as you begin to contemplate, to evaluate, to test, and to understand yourself — your lessons, and your patterns. Your life and how you live it are of the utmost importance. Learning and growing are necessities. I urge you to take action to understand yourself better and to come closer and closer to finding your eternal being. Engage in your own vision quest.

"Many of the Indians believed that one may be born
more than once, and there were some who claimed to
have full knowledge of a former incarnation."

The Soul of the Indian, Copyright 1911,
by Charles Alexander Eastman
Artist: Diane Coleman

Chapter V

Self-Hypnosis and Ideals (Inner Adventure)

A. Ideals: A Practical Standard of Excellence

The evaluation of ideals is an important part of our work with patterns. Patterns reflect our ideals of the past, and our current ideals create future patterns.

Recognition of the need for ideals offers an invitation to explore your mind, your reasons, and purposes for living. We use our ideals to evaluate important things in our lives. Often, this is done unconsciously. At an inner level we weigh circumstances, decisions, and goals by our ideals. We ask ourselves, "Is it in line with my ideal, or against my better good?"

The motivating force behind – and actually, in the forefront of – our actions is our ideals which might change and grow as we mature. Ideals are on physical, mental, emotional, and spiritual levels, and their development is in accord with our learning on each level.

Sometimes we seem to have opposing ideals. For example, a spiritual ideal might be the decision to meditate for an hour daily, simply for the benefit of the spiritual balance which it brings. On the other hand, a physical need requires us to work long hours at a job in order to earn enough money to feed our families, and to pay our bills. Both are valid and positive ideals.

The solution might be to compromise and to allow less than an hour for meditation, but also to take some time out from the heavy work schedule. Other valid solutions might exist as well. In either case, the ideal governs how we invest our time and our energy for what we deem to be the expansion of Self.

The central force in life – the over-riding principle, the guiding light – reflects our ideals. The vision of ourselves that surpasses our ordinary selves, our pattern of excellence, and our highest purpose, all indicate what we hold as IDEAL. Personality is a reflection of ideals and character.

The Edgar Cayce readings helped to express this concept by advising people to maximize the virtues and minimize the faults. This does not mean to look only for the good while pretending the faults are absent, but rather to focus more fully on the good that it may grow still more. The ideal is a conception of *you* in your *perfection*.

Kahlil Gibran, writing in one of the most widely known and beautiful books of our age, *The Prophet*, delivers the same concept:

"Of the good in you I can speak, but not of the evil.
You are good when you walk to your goal firmly
  and with bold steps.
Yet you are not evil when you go thither limping.
Even those who limp go not backward.

In your longing for your giant self lies your good-
ness: and that longing is in all of you."

Gibran also explains how we may have conflicting
goals and purposes. "For a divided house is not a den
of thieves; it is only a divided house." He proceeds to
suggest the importance of establishing an ideal, which
he likens to the rudder of a ship that keeps your life
"on course."

Cayce's source focused often on ideals, reminding
us that the real ideals are *within*, and that there is a
great difference between being good, and in being good
for something. He counseled people to find self, *first*.
Know in *whom* and in *what* they believe in order to
make their lives constructive. Know *what* you believe
and *why* you believe it. Begin with self, for Self is the
best help.

There are few rules regarding what constitutes an
ideal. Ideals are as varied as the people who hold
them. *Living* your ideal is different from *having* an
ideal. The living requires work and commitment.
Stand firmly for your ideals. Someone has said, "If you
don't stand for something, you'll fall for anything." Set
a higher ideal than everyone expects of you. Set the
highest ideal you can *possibly* set for yourself.

There is, moreover, a difference between goals and
ideals. A rather big difference. A goal is what we wish
to achieve; the ideal is the motive behind it. We might
have goals of developing psychic ability, or managing
our stress, or overcoming insomnia – things we strive
for. Now, *why* do we want those abilities? Do we want
psychic ability to be able to show off to our friends, or
to help humanity with the gift? If we want it to gain

KAHLIL GIBRAN

SEEKING THE SILENCE

Artist: Julia Freeman

foresight and to help in our spiritual development, fine; but, if we merely flaunt this ability it can prove to be a major stumbling-block in our lives. The *reasons* we want things are of the utmost importance. They are vital clues to our ideals.

Cayce's source stressed that ideals are not to be confused with goals. An ideal may be a principle or a person whom we use as a model because he or she lives according to the principles we wish to strengthen. *Find self first. Know in whom and in what you believe,* the source cautioned. One might choose Mother Teresa or Elizabeth Kubler-Ross as an ideal of a life to emulate. Another might choose Jesus or Ghandi to emulate or to learn from. Some might even choose a favorite relative.

One might select a basic physical goal, such as losing weight with the motivation of looking better, improving one's general health, or protecting, specifically, the heart and vital organs. Such goals might, in the long run, serve a higher spiritual ideal if we wish to maintain good health in order to pursue our own higher growth, and to be more productive in terms of sharing that growth with the world. Similarly, those with mental ideals might pursue further education in order to develop their minds and to avoid stagnation.

Many people develop spiritual ideals by meditation and prayer, by communion with their higher selves, or spirit guides. There are many levels of ideals. There are personal ideals, community ideals, national ideals, and planetary ideals. Who could deny the validity and importance of working toward world peace, or ecological and environmental balance, as a commendable planetary ideal.

In this first guided session you can focus on your personal ideals. Keep in mind that your ideal is the central motivating force of your life. It is your vision of yourself that surpasses the ordinary you. It is your pattern of excellence, your highest purpose.

First we formulate our ideals and then apply them to our lives; therefore, study your ideals and then seek to apply those principles. To "apply" means to use, or do, utilizing whatever is available to you. Jesus said, "By their fruits ye shall know them." That means that you shall be known by your actions and your works – not by your version of your life story, or your pro-spectus, or financial statements – but by *what you do*. First, search out with whom or what you have placed your ideal, and then put those ideals into action.

Cayce's source suggested that if we spiritualize and visualize purposes in the manner in which we desire things to be done, we shall have them done! Then the source advises, recommending the use of hypnosis to aid in applying the ideals: "(this) ... may be best done by suggestive forces to the body through hypnosis...." (3483-1) and "...In other words, put the body under what is commonly called hypnotic influence to bring about the normal condition of the action of the body itself...." (4506-1)

Self-hypnosis, by itself, can do very little for you except to bring you to your natural level of relaxation and comfort. What *is beneficial* is what you *do* while at that level! It is the Program, or the series of sugges-tions and visualizations, that brings accomplishment and success.

Self-hypnosis is just the first step in an entire program! In the same way, reading this book is a first step.

To gain fully, you must perform the activities – complete the tasks, do your work of self-improvement. Reading alone does not do it, but application *does*.

Hypnosis has been called "Mind Dynamics," or, by Dr. Herbert Benson, "The Relaxation Response," and several other things; but basically it *is* Self-Hypnosis, by which means we bring ourselves to a natural level of relaxation.

This process of self-hypnosis is shown in the diagram, "A Model for Self-Hypnosis." We can simplify self-hypnosis by dividing it into four component parts. The first part is the train engine, or the Relaxation, the first step in self-hypnosis.

In relaxation, there are four levels of brain-wave activity. The normal waking level is called *beta.* The *alpha* state is the beginning of self-hypnosis and the beginning of meditation; it is the level at which most people remain while in hypnosis. If, however, they have been working with relaxation techniques for some time, they probably will move to the next deeper level, called *theta.*

The alpha level is completely natural. We each experience this level at least twice daily: as we go to sleep at night, and as we come out of sleep in the morning. In effect, this means we have all been in self-hypnosis. Research shows that we may enter *alpha* several times throughout the day as we become engrossed in a book, as we daydream, or as we watch television. Statistics now show that, two thirds of the time, people watching television have entered into an *alpha* state. Why is this?

Television uses what may be termed "electronic"

hypnosis. It uses primarily visual images (visualization), and spoken words of suggestion. This combination makes it the perfect medium for hypnosis, for it engages both right and left hemispheres of the brain simultaneously.

This is only one example of how hypnosis is *already* in our lives, oftentimes without our awareness of it. Each of us experiences *alpha* which leads to deeper level *theta*, which is deep hypnosis, deep meditation, and also sleep. Furthermore, at every ninety-minute cycle, most of us move into the *delta* range, the third and final level of the deep sleep mode, or "quality" sleep time.

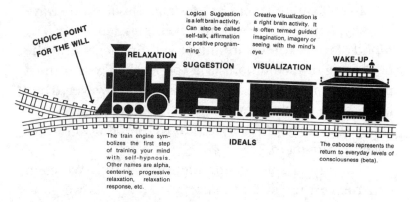

A MODEL FOR SELF-HYPNOSIS

It is important to emphasize here that self-hypnosis is not, in itself, an end, but rather the *primary tool* to help you to reach your natural alpha level of relaxation, which, in turn, enables you to be receptive to suggestion and to visualization exercises. The two latter terms are represented in the diagram by the two boxcars: Suggestion (the left brain activity of logic) and

Visualization (the right brain property of inspiration and creative genius).

In the model for self-hypnosis, the two boxcars represent the right and left hemispheres of the brain. This is the real work of any self-help session, to utilize a full brain approach, thus enlarging your mind's potential.

The left brain is associated with linear, logical thought. It covers information, analysis, details, grammar, and language. It recognizes the parts of things, and processes items one by one. For example, studying the various components of the train model is a left hemisphere activity. The left brain remembers complicated sequences of actions and it works with established rules, bringing form and order to our work.

The right brain perceives the whole picture; it recognizes the forest (not the single trees). It sees an overall design or a larger plan, usually by means of pictures or emotions. The right hemisphere responds to rhythmic patterns of prose, poetry, or song. Most of all, it is fresh, innovative and creative, bringing a new vision to our work.

When scientists have found it necessary to dissect half a brain because of a tumor or the presence of some other condition, they have found that the healthy half of the brain has taken over the tasks of the impaired half. There is much debate regarding the workings of the human brain but, for simplicity's sake, study of the two hemispheres enables us to understand the different functions.

There are many books on the market which deal with creative visualization. There are also many books about positive suggestion and its benefits, as well as the use of affirmation and self-talk in our lives. Unfortunately, there are few books which can instruct us as to how we may combine both hemispheres and so empower the mind to build our lives the way we want them to be.

When you begin to make your own tapes for self-hypnosis, be sure to include exercises for both hemispheres – the left-brain "positive suggestion," and the right-brain "visualization." During this session you will guide yourself into alpha level, then proceed with those suggestions and visualizations you wish to reinforce. After the session, wake-up procedures are vitally important – just as important as those which allow you to enter the self-hypnotic state.

Self-hypnosis is not sleep. People only *appear* to be asleep; actually, the person is fully aware of everything that is going on. You will be in complete control at every level of your mind to accept, or to reject, anything. You will be aware of everything that is going on, and you will remember everything.

Some have asked, "Why, in stage demonstration, do people return to their seats unable to remember all the crazy things they did on stage?" This behavior was not caused by the hypnosis itself. It occurred because of a suggestion given by the stage entertainer to the volunteers, so that they would not be embarrassed by anything they had done once they returned to their seats. Hypnosis does not *create* amnesia, nor anesthesia. They result from suggestion. When suggestions are given to any person, that person must *accept* them in order for them to be effective. It is just as possible that the individual may reject them.

Now let us proceed to the topic of wake-up procedures. Wake-up procedure is actually a "coming out" procedure. The term "wake-up" is, however, the way most people think of it.

While experiencing self-hypnosis, some people progress into a sleep mode. If you find that you have a tendency to fall asleep – especially when using your tapes at night – sit up during the process. This usually will solve the problem. Remember, the greater benefits of self-hypnosis exercises (suggestions and visualizations) are best derived while fully aware and not at a night-time sleep level. In other words, while you are aware in alpha, and *only* while aware, can you repeat the suggestions mentally, and actively perform the visualizations. Nothing, of course, is wasted in sleep; but when we use self-hypnosis, taking a more active part in it proves to be much more effective.

Excellent courses in self-hypnosis are being taught, but the word "hypnosis" is seldom used. Why is this so? Surveys have shown that many people have a negative reaction to the *word*, but not to the process. They enjoy the relaxation, they enjoy the process, and they do very well with it. They retain a negative reaction to the term, however, because of the strange connotations it has garnered by dramatized and fictionalized misuse. The very *word* "hypnosis" frightens some people.

Even today, if you have a headache and have to choose from two remedies on the drugstore shelf – one labelled Acetylsalicylic Acid and one labelled Aspirin – which would you choose? Probably the latter, because it is much less intimidating than a remedy with "acid" in its name; yet, Acetylsalicylic Acid and Aspirin are one and the same. Aspirin is the same substance marketed under a different name. We are all aware of the importance of marketing in our society. There are brand names and there are generics. You might say that "hypnosis" is the generic term for all the off-shoot catch phrases.

A book called *Self-Talk*, for instance, is geared toward the business sector. It expounds the techniques that hypnotists have been teaching for years, but under new terminology. There is no mention of the word "hypnosis," not even in the appendix. The author is simply marketing the same principles in a new package. This is good marketing practice. If people have a negative reaction to one package, why try to re-educate the masses? Why not just re-package?

B. Mind Management

One of the most familiar expressions from Cayce's forty three years of readings was: **Spirit is the life; mind is the builder; the physical is the result.** Everything we have made or built in the physical world began in someone's mind. Somewhere in time, everything started in someone's imagination. **Mind is the builder.**

We all have had this feeling of consciously wanting something and pushing our lives in that direction. Another part of us pushes – at times – in the other direction, toward our subconscious desires. We are not robots; we can program our lives the way we want them to be. Because we are human, however, there is a time lapse from the programming to the manifestation into our reality. For some, this gap could be a few minutes or a few days; for others, it could be a few months, or even years. It is very different for everybody, and much depends upon how much we *really* want it subconsciously. Often, we only think we want it.

The value of self-hypnosis is that it enables us to unify our subconscious desires with our conscious desires. As the diagram illustrates, with both subconscious and conscious pushing the will together in the same direction, our life is guided in the direction we want it to go. Although this is a simplified version, it does explain the integration of conscious mind with the subconscious.

Without even realizing it, the conscious mind and the unconscious desires sometimes work against each other – pushing in opposite directions.

| **Your Conscious** | **Your subconscious** |
| **thinking mind** | **feeling mind** |

This results in a lot of effort with little accomplishment. The will to succeed is stuck. Sadly, your goals and desires may not be congruent with your words and actions.

Using self-hypnosis, you can synchronize your (known) conscious purposes with your subconscious (hidden) patterns.

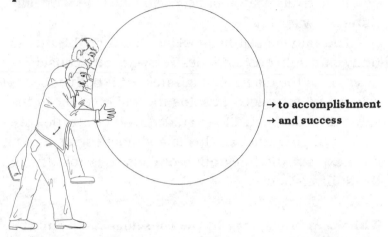

→ to accomplishment
→ and success

Your Conscious   **Your subconscious**
thinking mind   **feeling mind**

As your conscious ideals and subconscious desires unite to work together, – pushing and building in the same direction, there is no limit to what you can do.

MIND AS THE BUILDER
Artist: Jeffrey Winchester

C. The Journey Inward

There is no "best time," in a general sense, to use self-hypnosis tapes. Timing is very individual. The best time for *you* is at the high-time of your day. Pay attention to your circadian rhythms, or biological clock. If you reach your peak at around 10:00 a.m., that would be the best time for you. It may not, however, be practical if – for instance – you must be at work at that time. In that case, you will have to determine another time when you can profit best from the tapes. They may be used as often as you like.

What is the difference between self-hypnosis and meditation? The levels are the same, alpha and theta, but there is a difference. In meditation we generally open ourselves to guidance coming to us at the conscious level from a higher level of consciousness, the subconscious or superconscious. Symbolically, we open ourselves to guidance and to inspiration from our own higher mind, which is an eternal and everlasting source. In self-hypnosis, we focus the conscious mind and use it as a tool to instruct and to guide the unconscious in the direction that we consciously want our lives to go. The difference lies in how we *use* the alpha and theta levels, and not in the levels themselves. Meditation can be likened to a telescope looking out into the vastness of space. Self-hypnosis can be symbolized by a microscope focusing in on a specific goal or objective.

MEDITATION IS PERCEIVING A LARGER VIEW.

**SELF-HYPNOSIS HELPS TO FOCUS IN ON A
SPECIFIC GOAL OR OBJECTIVE.**

If this is your first time working with self-help or
self-hypnosis programs, you may wish to read, first,
about the field. Self-hypnosis is a safe, 100% natural
and direct way to improve your life. My book, *Self-
Hypnosis – Creating Your Own Destiny*, can help you
to gain a deeper knowledge of this science and the art
of hypnosis. (See back of this book).

The art of self-hypnosis concerns timing, tone,
and delivery – not going too fast or too slow, being too
forceful or too meek. The inner mind responds very
differently from the conscious mind. It contains profound depth and wisdom, yet, it works slowly and
requires clear, simple questions or instructions. It has
a natural simplicity and honesty, and is uncompli-
cated in its approach. Speak s-l-o-w-l-y, very slowly,

less than half your normal pace; even *slower* is best. Some people say they don't like the sound of their own voices on cassette tape. Paradoxically, the very apparatus that you don't like is the very tool that will help you. It may sound ironic, but you could work with your cassette recorder, in the privacy of your room, and practice speaking differently. If you have a high pitch, speak lower or deeper. If you mumble, begin to speak distinctly. If you normally speak in a monotone, add life and enthusiasm to your voice. Do whatever is necessary to improve the pitch, modulation, and speed of your voice. In just an hour or even less you will have improved the quality of your voice.

The good news is that you TRUST your own voice more than other voices. And, as you learned to improve your voice in the DOING (not just reading about it), so also you will learn best about self-hypnosis – in the doing. Theory is fine, but there is no substitute for practical experience.

You are ready now to make *your own* self-help, self-hypnosis tape. Get a cassette recorder with a good microphone and a blank tape. To record, find a place where you will not be distracted for about half an hour. First, read the following script aloud and make any changes, deletions, or additions which suit your personal preferences. Now read the script slowly into your cassette tape. Use your watch and time the one-minute pauses for one FULL minute. The inner mind needs that much time to process the question and give you the information requested.

In time, when you become more proficient at making self-hypnosis tapes, you can add the sound of a grandfather-clock ticking in the background, or the soothing music of one of the "Old Masters," or the gentle sounds of the "New Age" genre.

Once your tape is completed, find another quiet time to enjoy using your tape. Self-hypnosis relaxes the body, builds the mind, and energizes your life in amazing and wonderful ways. It is a "win-win-win" activity with great benefit to be gained and no downside. Remember to breathe deeply throughout the session, for deep breathing is one of the oldest and most effective methods of relaxation.

Use your tape more than once if you wish, perhaps as often as once a week during the coming month. Keep a journal or diary, and log-in the results. Describe whatever you receive: what did you see, what did you feel, what did you hear, what did you perceive? For some people, the information is fleeting, as in a dream. For others, it comes clearly and strongly. There is no right or wrong method for receiving and processing information; whatever you receive is correct for you, and will improve over time and with experience and patience.

You may use your tape for yourself and share it with friends and family. (Better still, teach them to make their own tapes!) You may also read the script aloud to loved ones if a recorder is not available. If you, or they, do not like the word "hypnosis" you may substitute any other appropriate words you prefer. Some term this kind of work a "guided reverie," an "inspired meditation," or a "working dream."

In fact, let's term these sessions an "inner adventure" which allows you, or others, to experience it without pre-conceptions or pre-conditions. It *is* simply – and profoundly – an inner spiritual adventure. You can experience as much of the adventure (or as little) as YOU wish.

Be gentle with yourself, be kind to your mind! *Whatever* you receive in your session is a gift from your subconscious mind. If you accept and welcome that gift, then, surely, more will be given another time. If you criticize your inner mind and negate or belittle your gift, you limit your potential.

TRUST is the key to the door of spiritual growth, and APPRECIATION makes the opening easier. BE THANKFUL for all that you receive and you will gain and grow as you journey the spiritual path, both by clarifying your Ideals and by experiencing other sessions yet to come!

D. An Ideals Inner Adventure
(Begin to record your tape here)

As soon as you are ready, ask yourself to close your eyes. If you take a deep breath, you can feel your body relaxing. As you slow your breathing, you let your mind relax.

Begin by comparing your mind to the surface of a quiet pond. My voice can be as a breeze whispering in the trees along the shore. The pond remains smooth and calm, even though things go on beneath the surface. There may be much happening beneath a still surface. The gentle surface conceals an extraordinary depth. Reflect upon nature, its beauty and elegance.

(Pause, one minute)

Now it is easy to dissolve this image and to form another – perhaps a stairway leading down – you can

see yourself leisurely descending. The stairs are covered with a thick, plush carpet, a carpet that is like a
cloud beneath your feet. Perhaps there is a brass
handrail or a walnut banister. The stairs lead you to
a ballroom with sparkling crystal chandeliers, or to a
comfortable room with books and crackling logs in a
fireplace. And while you are here, the outside world
will *stay* outside. You can take a few minutes and
notice just how good you feel here.

(Pause, one minute)

You can do anything you want to do. You don't
even have to listen to my voice, because your subconscious hears with new awareness and responds all by
itself.

You are now learning to recognize the feelings that
accompany inner relaxation. You may experience a
light, medium, or deep level of relaxation; you choose
what is best for you. Your body may feel heavy or it
may feel light, or it may seem to be asleep so that it
doesn't feel anything at all. It may float up, or it may
sink down, or it may very pleasantly drift. It may do
whatever you wish. Perhaps your body feels as if it has
gone to sleep even though your mind seems to be
awake. Of course, you don't have to concern yourself
with that.

This is a learning and growing experience. Of
course, you may go very deep – and safely. Your inner
mind is aware; it knows when it needs to respond and
can do so in just the right way. It already has gained
more awareness.

If I count from ten to one, then you may go deeper
– more in perfect harmony – by picturing yourself

descending a flight of stairs, or going down in an elevator or on an escalator – any pleasant image that you wish.....ten, nine, eight, seven, six, five, four, three, two, one.

And if I count from ten to one again, you may go twice as deep, enjoying a pleasant, comfortable feeling – any sort of feeling that you wish.....ten, nine, eight, seven, six, five, four, three, two, one.

As you relax, take a deep breath, and slow down, you may go even deeper. As you enjoy the comfort, you will note that there is less and less importance to my voice. You may find yourself drifting in your own ideal, joyful place of relaxation.

(Pause, one minute)

Now we can begin a series of exercises using the Creative Imagination and Positive Affirmation. In your mind, now, you may begin constructing a box. This box may be of any size, any shape, any dimension, any color, or any material that you wish.

Make a lid for your box, but not a lock. I will be quiet now, so that you may construct your box. Then, when I begin to speak again, you can take a deep breath and go deeper. Build your box now.

(Pause one full minute, or longer)

Take a deep breath and go deeper...more in perfect harmony. Now, open the lid to your box and carefully place in this box all of your cares, all of your concerns, all of your worries, your hopes, your expectations, your fears. Place them safely in the box – whether actually or symbolically, full size or in miniature, or even written on little pieces of paper. Whatever you choose to do is correct for you. And as you place all your concerns safely into the box, I will be quiet.

(Pause, one minute)

Now, when you are ready, gently close the lid on your concerns, but do not lock the box. And, as you put the box aside, the following words echo deeply, within your mind:

"An ideal is a central motivating force in life. It is a vision of self that surpasses the ordinary self. It is a pattern of excellence, the highest purpose, character, and integrity.

A goal is something to be achieved in life. An ideal is much more important; it is the deeper, underlying reason related to the goal. An ideal is often private and sacred — the most positive, and often hidden, motive and purpose.

An ideal is a standard or measure to assess activity. It is a long-term investment in life.

(Pause)

Now, I am going to ask a series of questions that you can answer from deep within. Allow the answers to come from deep within and accept the information you are given:

What do you **REALLY** want to do with your life, and why?

(Pause, one minute)

What are you doing in your life that is working well?

(Pause, one minute)

What are your greatest strengths?

(Pause, one minute)

How would you act, even if you were certain you'd never be found out or get blamed?

(Pause, one minute)

How would you act, even if you were certain you'd never receive any credit or recognition?

(Pause, one minute)

What are the strongest POSITIVE PATTERNS you have noticed in your life?

(Pause, one minute)

What are the most CHALLENGING PATTERNS you have worked with?

(Pause, one minute)

Whom do you hold as an ideal – someone living or dead whom you admire or respect? Why is this person important to you?

(Pause, one minute or more)

And now, just imagine that you are wearing a T-shirt which can have a message printed upon it. In a moment I will ask you to write or to print a specific message on the front of your T-shirt, a short sentence or a few words in answer to this question:

"What was your mother's message to you?" (Note: If you do not know your biological mother, substitute a person who filled the "mother role." In other sessions, the father may be substituted for the mother). "What did she say, or convey to you countless times, in countless ways, whether spoken or unspoken?" Write that message to you on the front of your T-shirt.

(Pause, one minute or more)

Now, on the back of your T-shirt, write or print your answer. How do you respond to your mother's message? Write this on the back of your T-shirt.

(Pause, one minute)

Now, your mother's message on the front of your T-shirt can give you insight into HER ideals for you – her fears, her hopes, her concerns, her prayers for you.

(Short pause)

Your answer on the back gives you insight into your ideals, your purposes, your direction for self.

(Short pause)

Remember those messages that you may bring them back with you later. Remember ALL the information that you have been given here today – the gifts from your inner guidance. You may wish to leave the cares and concerns safely in the box and to return to them later, whenever you wish.

You have done so very well here today. I will count slowly from one to ten. At the count of ten you may open your eyes and be wide awake.

One: coming up slowly.

Two: remember what you have been given here today.

Three: total normalization at every level of your being.

Four: you may wish to move hands, or feet, or neck.

Five.

Six.

Seven: coming up to your full potential.

Eight: revitalized.

Nine: re-energized.

Ten: open your eyes and wide awake now. Wide awake!

E. An Ideals Project

Now that you have experienced the IDEALS inner adventure, it's time to recall and to utilize the information received. In the process of writing, you will probably recall even more of the information. This may sound odd, but it's true. Technically, it's called "writing to learn," and it helps people to get more out of their experiences. It is thinking on paper! In the writing, you will discover interesting connections and will observe new processes; your understanding will broaden, you'll ask questions, and then proceed to answer them yourself! So let's get started. We'll call this an "I-D-E-A-L-S" project! And you'll remember it with this anagram:

1. Identify the ideal _____.

2. Describe the situation, and challenges_____.

3. Explore possible solutions or actions to strengthen the ideal _____.

4. Act upon the information; what can you start doing? _____.

5. Look for results; imagine them already accomplished _____.

6. Save the information for future analysis and study

When you answer the questions and work with the material you WILL have found an IDEALS solution!

Writing, speaking, and listening are the important tools for learning. Take time, every day if possible, and write in your journal or diary. Write any inspirations that come to you concerning your ideals. Sometimes the greatest inspirations come as a fleeting thought, or are triggered by an event. Grab that thought as it whizzes by – it may be exceedingly valuable to you.

What did you receive or perceive in this session that surprised you?_____.

F. Notes to Remember Regarding Self-Hypnosis

1. The best way to learn anything is in the *doing* of it. You will learn far more by making your *own tapes*, for instance, than by using commercial tapes that someone else has made. Of

course, you may purchase or borrow commercial tapes from bookstores, pharmacies, libraries, and by mail order to learn different approaches to the subject.

2. Next, I recommend that you study the excellent material from the Edgar Cayce readings under the titles of "Suggestive Therapeutics," and "Mind: The Builder." I also suggest that you study books by and about Dr. Milton H. Erickson, on whose methods the Neuro Linguistic Programming (NLP) courses are based. Erickson was the first to teach that all hypnosis *is* self-hypnosis.

3. Incorporate what you learn from Cayce, Erickson, and your other readings into *your own* self-help, positive programming tapes. Soon, people will notice important and profound changes in your life and will ask you (directly or indirectly) the reason for those changes. When you start to radiate new light, people always notice it! Explain to them about self-help tapes and show them how to make their own. The goal is to learn personal empowerment, not power over others.

4. A course in hypnosis is another option toward achieving personal transformation. Many community colleges offer such courses at a modest cost. Atlantic University in Virginia Beach, VA., offers excellent certificate courses on the subject of hypnosis. Remember, all you need for this study are high ideals and a sincere desire for personal improvement. Even a small amount of time invested now pays off later in

big dividends.

5. The most exciting and inexpensive way to learn hypnosis is to start a small study group. It is easy, productive, and *fun*. Simply find a friend or two, and start an informal study group. Meet once a month at home, or in a library conference room. Often, meeting rooms are free when meetings are open to the public. You may place free announcements in your newspaper calendar section or on radio community bulletins. New people will hear of your work and will attend. Here are some tips for starting your hypnosis study group:

   (a) A small group of even two or three people working together is more influential than two or three dozen people working alone. Meeting together on a regular basis produces great accomplishment.

   (b) Your group may have a different moderator each meeting. Start with the study of traditional areas of hypnosis and branch out into the more innovative and newer methods. This is a "learn as you study and share" approach.

   (c) An established group can invite guest speakers. Occasionally, you may ask a professional in some related field to speak. Most are pleased to do this. Soon you may start to guide sessions for individuals or for the entire group itself. Of course, this is a bit harder at first as you realize that you are all amateurs and still learning. But "amateur" comes from the root-word meaning "love:" that is, you love this study and this work.

(d) In your love of learning, you begin to reach out and to inspire others – helping others to help themselves. Then, as the months fly by, you and your group will begin to realize that you have educated yourselves in a personal and profound manner. You have "drawn-out" what was already there deep within yourselves; and having brought it out, you've shared your light with others.

(e) From the seeds of small study groups (as Christ explained about the mustard seed) in time and with patience – with care and nurturing – the great plants of spiritual fulfillment grow. Your study group may not enlighten the entire planet, but it will bring light to illuminate your own area. It is said that if you wish to plant for days, plant flowers; if you wish to plant for years, plant trees; but it you wish to plant for eternity, plant ideas. And IDEALS. Begin now to search inward for your highest self!

Chapter VI

Embracing Your Eternal Child (Inner Adventure)

A. Your Inner Child Learns

Almost all researchers, teachers, psychologists and parents agree that most of our patterns and behaviors are linked directly to our youth. Even the first few months and years of life have profound bearing on the rest of our lives. With this understanding, you can glimpse how important this chapter will be for you in understanding the foundations of your current life.

How did you do with the Ideals Inner Adventure? If you have not made and used your tape, please do so now. If you received only a little information, please wait a few days and use your tape another time. If you received valuable insight and information, USE that in whatever ways it can help you. Write the information in your journal, sketch the messages on your T-shirt.

We have come a long way together and have learned much. Learning comes in two ways: ACTIVE and REFLECTIVE modes. Participating in the exercises in this book helps you to accomplish both.

ACTIVE LEARNING is in doing things, and is

often called "hands-on" work. Examples are in the making and using of your Inner Adventure tapes, going on a retreat for a weekend, or involvement with a study or support group.

REFLECTIVE LEARNING takes place when you pause for a few moments (or a few days) and ponder what you are learning. Journal writing and withdrawing into your spiritual sanctuary are reflective exercises. Rest and silence are vital to learning as it helps in the assimilation of experiences. Pauses and spaces are very important in the same way that spaces between the words on this page make it easier to read the words, and to comprehend the thoughts. (Aspacemakesitmucheasier!)

Sometimes our active and reflective learnings overlap. Learning is not always sequential; it is erratic and comes in leaps and bounds. There are quiet times of rest and reflection mixed with active times of challenge and endurance. There is a rhythm to the process of learning. Learning is growing - and, often, growing involves pain and anxiety.

Although pauses and rest are necessary, in a general sense, growing is better than not growing, good learning is better than not learning, and wise-action is better than stagnation. Dilemmas and challenges can lead to resolutions. Even failure can bring valuable learning. Difficult lessons may later produce profound accomplishment. It is possible to learn from all of life's experiences. Even tragedies can lead to growth. Adversity need not be an end; it can be a beginning.

As humans in the continuing saga called "life," we learn and grow in numerous ways. Perhaps the best metaphor for our many grades and classes would be

OFTEN, WE ARE OUR OWN BEST TEACHERS
Artist: Jeffrey Winchester

a school — a vast School of Life. This school — let's call it Earth School — is like a vocational school in practical learning and application. There are rules, there is some theorizing, but, primarily, it is a place of experience and activity.

In our metaphor, this school is unique because we are all students AND teachers, at different levels of learning. Those who graduate go on to further realms. The rest of us continue to learn - hopefully! To me, the very fact that we are enrolled suggests that we still have something to learn — or to teach.

Many people ask, "What is the purpose of this Earth School?" For that I cannot give a definitive response. Yet, I do feel that we are here to EXPERIENCE life - all of life, with its benefits and its struggles, its highs and its lows. Our courses blend blessing and challenge, struggle and success, grand opportunities and subtle simplicities.

For example, a few students may be engaged in a philosophical debate: "Is the glass of water half-full or half-empty? This may seem a ponderous question for some, but other students drink and enjoy the glass of water. They ponder not how full or not-full it may be; they wholeheartedly drink of the cool, refreshing water. Those are the students who live the experience; those are the adventurous ones.

The most adventuresome students choose a self-directed course of study. True education means to "draw out" what is already within oneself. When we go deep into our own minds, we can discover our hidden talents and abilities, our patterns and potentials. This course of study can be very rewarding, but it requires self-discipline and courage.

Self-education has no bounds or limits! Each day becomes an adventure in learning, with discoveries which can bring pain, but also joy! Our world is an unlimited opportunity for the self-motivated and self-determined student. Travel in this world may well be one of the most valuable lessons in Earth School curriculum. Venturing beyond what we know challenges our courage, values and adaptability. It offers adventure and invitation to mystical experiences.

When you travel upon this wondrous Earth, be sure to go to the sacred places where other students and teachers from times past have built centers and shrines. This will help to connect you to your ancient past — and open possibilities to your future. Take pilgrimages to the holy centers of humanity and see the wonders created by nature. Wander in reverence throughout the lands, among the peoples, and fully ENJOY the adventure.

B. Reflections in the Face of Time

In times of reflection, study the lives of spiritual leaders, saints and mystics; perhaps they can be as mentors to you through their writings and examples. Though their legacy is of courage and strength, you may also find that their lives were fraught with struggle and pain. Hurt and suffering may have been a necessary ingredient — or even the catapult — to spiritual heights. This pattern is a common factor with holy women and men throughout time, and from all lands and civilizations.

Spiritual courses hold little — if any — personal glory in a wordly sense. Certainly, *after* their death

**TAKE TIME FOR REFLECTION IN THE
PRIVACY OF YOUR SOUL**
Artist: Jeffrey Winchester

some spiritual leaders are recognized and revered, but during their lives the opposite is more often the rule. And for every recorded life of a spiritual leader (whether in story or in legend), there may be hundreds who lived, did great works, and died virtually unknown. Though history may fail to record their lives, it IS stored and recorded in the deep memory of that person, and within those people who were touched, helped, or healed by that one. The lesson — love and giving — is what is most important, not necessarily a paragraph in a history book.

Perhaps those spiritual leaders were just too far ahead of us, and of their time. Some challenged the political establishments of their era. Others questioned the temporal religious powers, and were branded as witches or heretics. Though the spiritual path be a lonely and desolate trek at times, there are sublime moments of enlightenment and wonder.

As challenging or as easy as your spiritual journey may be, it is the BEST course to help you to graduate from Earth School into the University of Eternity.

C. Preparing for Your Next Adventure

In this Earth School, perhaps you are ready for your next lesson, your next homework project. This assignment is to help you to make a better connection with your inner child. There is, deep within you and within every other person, a timeless aspect — your eternal self. This part of you reaches far beyond the boundaries of time. Each person also has an inner quality of wisdom and strength, beyond the limits of present time and location.

This Inner Adventure will assist you in making a stronger connection with those parts of you that are *already within*, and will draw them out for your benefit. This is not a session to work with psychological problems or to heal a "wounded" part of your youth. Did you have a happy childhood? Not everyone did; and sad to say, some people have no pleasant memories of their early years.

This guided adventure begins with remembering a time when you felt safe and comfortable. If you cannot find such a time in your memory, just imagine how wonderful it would be IF there had been such a time. You are not creating a "false memory," but rather using your constructive imagination to bring a feeling of safety and comfort — this feeling allows you to open yourself, to start trusting yourself and your inner guidance more carefully.

Use the guidelines from the previous Inner Adventure for making a cassette tape of the following script. After completing the session, fill in the analysis sheet that follows. Write in your journal about the insights and information that come to you, or from you. Even if the insight might be subtle, be sure to log it in; if information should flow in abundance, be thankful.

The Inner Adventure is designed for your personal use, but you may also read it to friends, to loved ones, or to a study group. Remember to time all pauses for one FULL minute (or more). Read the script slowly at one-third the usual rate of speech and read it distinctly.

THE INCREDIBLE HEALING POWER OF LOVE
Artist: Kathye Mendes

D. Embracing Your Eternal Child — The Incredible Healing Power of Love — An Inner Adventure

Before we start, make yourself comfortable so that you can relax and be at ease without distractions for about 40 minutes.

We will begin the exercise by taking two full minutes for you to relax, allowing you to use your favorite method of relaxation. If you have worked with Edgar Cayce's material, you may wish to use his head and neck exercises. If you've done any Yoga or deep breathing exercises, use those. If you have a favorite method of self-hypnosis, use it. If you do not have a favorite method, I suggest that you just remember a time when you *really* felt safe and comfortable. If you don't remember a time like that, just imagine how wonderful it would be if there had been a time when you truly felt safe, comfortable and at peace.

(Pause full two minutes)

Now, with your eyes closed, it becomes easier and easier for you to become more and more aware of a number of things that could often go overlooked or even unnoticed. Thoughts, feelings, sensations, impressions — just remember now to breathe deeply and smoothly, for deep breathing is one of the most ancient and also one of the most effective forms of relaxation there is. So remember to breathe deeply and smoothly throughout the entire exercise. Just allow yourself to drift pleasantly and easily. You don't have to think, or to move about, or to make any sort of effort. You don't even have to try to listen to me, because your subconscious is here and can hear every word. You are about to enter a magical realm — please leave all doubts safely behind — then proceed.

As you take another deep breath, just experience the *feeling* of letting go — just letting go. Becoming more in perfect harmony, more centered with every breath you take.

Can you remember being a child and going to school? (Pause) If you recall a pleasant, happy memory, your mouth automatically forms a little smile. A smile comes easily and naturally with the memory.

As a child, did you dream? Can you dream here again, as when you were a child? Perhaps in the dream, you may be walking along the shore by the water's edge with your bare feet in the sand. Feels cool, but good. Feel the warm sun shining on your skin; there is a cool breeze that balances the warmth of the sun. And there go the sea gulls. Are they laughing? Why not? Spontaneous joy and laughter. And as the dream continues, you also continue to go deeper and deeper, softly into the season of gentle dreams. Perhaps you may remember a special song or a tune from your childhood, and that song or tune echoes deep, deep within. Don't analyze your responses, just allow the tune or music to return pleasantly.

(Pause one minute)

If you don't recall a favorite song or tune from your youth or childhood, perhaps you can recall the tune and words of "Row, Row, Row Your Boat, Gently Down the Stream."

(Pause one minute)

The melody takes you even deeper within, deeper into your dream. And there is another dream within the dream. The dream of your eternal self, your eternal child. That carefree, innocent part of you — the part of you that is eager to learn, eager to experience, eager to grow, eager to love, to be loved. Connect now with your inner child, that joyful, wonderful, innocent part of you, and I will be quiet while you enjoy this experience.

(Pause one minute)

You may now even wish to communicate with your inner child, or to embrace this child and to experience the incredible healing power of love.

(Pause one minute)

Your child may even wish to give you a gift, something tangible or intangible — a word, a phrase — I don't know what your gift will be, but receive the gift now from your inner child.

(Pause one minute)

Hold your gift close, in fullness and thankfulness. You may even wish to wrap it around your heart so that you may keep it always. Thank your inner child for your gift.

Now as the dream progresses, you can continue to walk along the water's edge. In the innocence of the child are the wisdom and strength of the universe.

Now the dream beckons you to a river — the river of life — down through the shadows of millions of yesterdays flow the waters of a life everlasting. Now when you're ready, you may float upon the waters of life. And you go to the very source — to the headwa-

EMBRACING YOUR ETERNAL CHILD
Artist: Jeffrey Winchester

ters, the wellspring. Notice the air. It may be rarefied, but it leaves you with a feeling of wonderment. There is excitement here - and strength and wisdom, for this is the abode of your higher self, the very highest aspects of your being. Here is your holy woman or your wise man within — the sage, the counselor — the friend who watches over and helps you, guides you, and protects you — your most special and wonderful friend. Greet this holy man or wise woman within. You may wish to communicate with your mentor — so I will be quiet while you do so.

(Pause one minute)

You may even wish to embrace your wise counselor or mentor. Permission is given, and once again you experience the incredible healing power of love.

(Pause one minute)

This wise being also has a special gift for you. Receive your gift now from the holy man or the wise woman.

(Pause one minute)

Receive your gift in fullness and in thankfulness. Wrap it around your heart also, if you wish, so that you may bring it back with you. Now bid farewell to this spiritual being, with the understanding that you may return here at any time you desire.

And now the dream fades and melts into the river of life with its everlasting waters, and brings you into your very own home, or dwelling place. It feels good to be here — to be back. In your home or on your land, you may wish to create a special place, a sacred place for rest and repose — of relaxation and peace. How do

EMBRACING YOUR WISE WOMAN
Artist: Jeffrey Winchester

you do this? First, simply find a favorite place, a certain area or section that has a special meaning to you. Then, perhaps you can bring a candle or two, but even that is not necessary. Bring, perhaps, a shell that you once found — or someone gave you — from the seashore. Bring a special rock, a mineral or crystal. Bring a feather — bring anything you wish to your sacred place.

(Pause for one minute)

Surround yourself with the sacred objects of your life or reminders of other lives. Those sacred objects are called sacraments. Bring a picture of a friend or a loved one — a memento from some enchanted time or place — from a special vacation, perhaps. Bring a picture of a holy person, a sage, or a special healer. Bring a mirror so that you can look deeply into your soul. There are no rules; there are no regulations. When you create a family altar or a home temple, you bring whatever your heart inspires you to bring. Bring the gift that you just received from your inner child. Bring also the gift that you received from your inner counselor. And if you wish, you may bring a loved one or a special friend to your sanctuary — Angels may come also. If you build it, if you will it, they will come.

(Pause for one minute)

This private sanctuary is where you come to re-energize — to center yourself, to focus on your ideals. It feels good to come here. It is a place where you take time to enjoy and to have fun. So I will be quiet now, so that you may envision - or mentally create - your sacred sanctuary.

(Pause for one minute)

And just imagine that this is already accomplished — that you already have built your sacred and special place. Now the dream melts into another dream — a dream within a dream — which is in yet another dream, the dream we call "life." For is life not a dream?

And as you begin coming back from the dream, walking along the water's edge, the songs of your youth still echo deeply within. And it's sometimes hard to realize when one dream ends and another begins — just as when one life ends and another begins. In just a short while after your death in this current life, this life itself may seem like just a dream. What you perceive as reality may become nebulous and vague. Reality melts into the dream as dreams create your next reality. Even more amazing revelations may dawn in some future life. If you experience a regression in *that* life, you may wonder whether you are "just imagining" the current life.

Now it is time to begin returning to this interesting dream we call the present day — our current reality. Bring yourself up slowly. Bring back your special gifts. Bring back with you all that was helpful. Let the dreamer awaken. Just take all the time you wish.

E. Embracing Your Eternal Child — An Analysis

Writing the answers to these questions will bring further insights:

Now that you have completed this Inner Adventure, what are your feelings?

What did you bring back that can help you?

What did you process? What are your reflections?

Write what you'd like to investigate further. Would you like to talk to parents or any grandparents for confirmation of information?

What will you now DO with the information and insights?

What message and gift did your inner child give to you?

What was the message and gift of your mentor?

Will you actually build a home sanctuary or keep it at a symbolic level?

What did you receive in this session that you didn't expect to receive?

Chapter VII

The Soul's Remembrances (Inner Adventure)

A. All Things to Your Remembrance

As we approach the beginning of a new century – and a new millennium – a grass-roots revolution is taking place in human consciousness. It is a peaceful revolution in human potential and spiritual vision, a revolution in healing the whole person – beyond what we experience in the physical and mental realms – which reaches into the heart of a deeper reality. As a part of this revolution, brave new plans are birthing, old institutions are dying, entire nations are turning, and people everywhere are growing. Change is everywhere; almost everything and everyone is experiencing profound changes. What was once feared is now open to the light of day.

My work is an exploration deep into the very soul of humanity itself. I feel fortunate to be a part of this healing revolution. I am a past-life researcher, and as such, I would like to share my unique perspective of a quest for discovery.

When I began this strange and wonderful career, the title of "past-life researcher" did not exist. My early

goal to be a priest was nurtured as I grew up in a
Catholic family, even as was my sister who has been
a nun all of her adult life. We both were imbued with
the idea that we could help humanity in a spiritual
way. As a teenager and an avowed television watcher,
I decided that the life of a detective was for me. Although that was a goal happily never achieved, I have
discovered that I am actually a detective of sorts, in-
vestigating clues which involve the mysteries of time
and of the soul. I sincerely pray that my work helps
others to grow spiritually.

In spite of a thirty year search, I still have much
to learn. In fact, it seems that my search is still just
beginning. The secrets of the ages are not revealed in
the blink of an eye in cosmic time. During those years
I have gained much insight through exhaustive testing and research. Certain peak episodes have been
experienced which I would like to share with you.

The belief in past lives is centuries old; but, the
methods of testing and exploring this belief are modern. Edgar Cayce, probably the greatest psychic of
modern times – if not of all time – gave life readings
for hundreds of people. He is credited with hundreds
of psychic readings in which he stated that each of
those people had all experienced numerous lifetimes,
and most would return again and again to the physical world. In a few readings he said that a certain soul
had reached a proper state of development and need
not incarnate again.

While in a psychic trance he stated repeatedly that
we are far more than merely physical beings who possess a sense of identity or ego. He reported that we are
immortal, spiritual beings who, from time to time, tem-

porarily inhabit a physical body in the Earth plane. He suggested that an evaluation of one's past lives would enable one to make better progress in the current life.

B. Spiritual Pioneering

Modern hypnosis now presents us with a relatively new method to explore the "inner space" which includes the heart, the mind and the uncharted sanctuary of our deeper selves. Past-life researchers, using a "mind awake, body asleep" state of consciousness, work to bring out information and emotions that are already in one's mind. Hypnotists are not magicians; we put nothing in, but simply draw out what is already there. That information may come from the present life, a past life, or even life seen from a future perspective.

Bringing a past problem or pattern into awareness is the first step. That way it can be encountered honestly and released, solving the problem or changing the pattern. In some cases this can be accomplished in one or two sessions. Conversely, multiple sessions may be required to achieve complete success.

People vary widely in their responses to their first regression experience. The secret is in their level of trust. For some, the vision is clear. Emotions and feelings are strong; even hearing and smelling are acute. Pictures unfold easily. For others, it is like looking through a glass darkly. It may take several sessions for some to accept themselves fully.

In those sessions people begin to fit together the jigsaw pieces of their puzzled pasts. But even most importantly, they discover the positive patterns of their

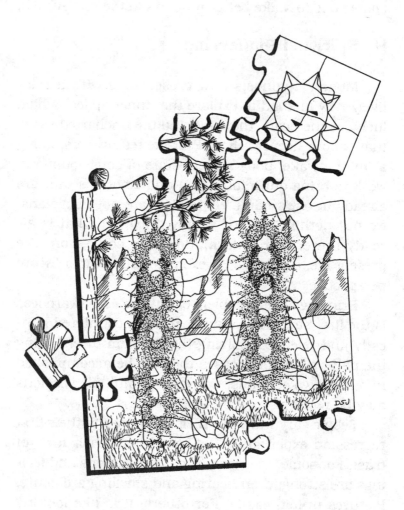

**REGRESSIONS PATIENTLY PIECE TOGETHER THE
PARTS OF A PUZZLING PAST
Artist: Sue Jones**

own pasts, their eternal gifts, and the wonderful talents waiting deep within which they may not have recognized. There is far more depth to the human mind than we can possibly imagine.

Past-life memories are like gifts from the inner mind, or pieces of a puzzle. Regressionists work like Sherlock Holmes. They are meticulous detectives who search and assemble the clues of time and place. As disciplined detectives, they decipher and decode the territory of mind and its long-term memory. With time and work, one may fit the pieces of the past together to form a full picture.

Such insight does not "prove" a past life (or lives) to anyone but themselves. Attempting to verify the authenticity of past lives is like trying to prove the existence of love. Most people would agree that love exists; yet, how can it be proven? Can you explain why you love someone? Which of the five senses can you rely upon for evidence? If you cannot prove the existence of love, does this stop you from experiencing it? Furthermore, is it necessary for you to believe in love in order to share its rewards? Of course not! The real question is not proof, but spiritual evolvement. Love, like past-life memory, is simply to experience and to enjoy – to study, to learn, to utilize, and to grow.

Our research is controversial because the implications are so profound. If, in fact, we do live numerous lives, then our present actions and insights take on far more importance in long-term reality. Many are not ready for this responsibility. Thus, it is much easier for them to discount the entire concept. Avoidance requires little effort; it is always easier to discredit than to study and to learn.

C. Critical Mind or Compassionate Soul?

There is good reason for skepticism in all fields of science and discovery; but, equally essential is the need to be open-minded. Debunkers always have decried those who assert that they have lived before as someone famous. In my three decades of active regression and past-life exploration, *not once* have I encountered a person who reported being famous (or infamous) in a past life. The recalled experiences are, most often, those of common people performing everyday activities and leading normal lives.

Authentic past-life exploration is the study of the history of individuals, replete with the events, struggles, accomplishments, creations, foibles, and adventures of humanity. Everything in human experience comes to light in regression. The soul may have grown during terrible times, or stagnated in the best of times. The interrelationships among people can be the driving force that connects all events. The greatest discovery is that, at the level of mind, all people everywhere are interconnected, and all are similarly connected to God.

Although numerous therapists in the mental health field are rightly impressed with the healing aspects of regression therapy, for me, it is still, primarily, a work of the soul and spirit – one of demonstrating God's great love for humanity. The immense popularity of past-life regression has been realized because people are discovering important new answers to ancient queries. The mind stands ready to yield great secrets, if relevant questions are asked. Each mind is like a time capsule – a vast treasure trove of wonder, experience and expression.

Who can benefit from regression or progression? Anyone who has ever asked those two questions which beg for answers: "What did I do to deserve *this*?", "Why am I going through this *again*?", questions which, up until now, have been purely rhetorical. Today, using modern hypno-regression techniques, we may begin a search for the answers to those questions. The search requires vision and foresight. It can reward us with great insight and understanding. In my own search, I have gained knowledge and experience, and have attempted to refine my own skills and techniques toward the purpose of helping to guide others in their quests for discovery. It is a work of great responsibility, requiring total integrity for mending hearts and minds, and for healing ancient wounds.

Reading about new possibilities gives purpose; studying gives knowledge. Applying knowledge, along with purpose, brings wisdom. Wisdom can be gained only through experience – not in a classroom, nor from books – but only in real-life lessons of "Earth School."

Beliefs once held as absolute truth in the past have changed as new knowledge is revealed. Unfortunately, there always will be those who, out of fear, ignorance, or foolishness, distrust new discoveries and resist change. Often, the very people who most loudly demand proof are those who adamantly refuse to see the truth when it is there before their eyes.

As we continue this great work of discovery, we must acknowledge all those pioneers who have gone courageously before us. It is with their spirit of adventure that we must strive to trace the pathways of the mind and to advance our understanding. Brave new

STUDYING THE PATTERNS

THE ADVENTURE OF LIFETIMES
Artist: Jeffrey Winchester

trails are being opened into the heart of our deeper reality. I encourage you to venture deeply within your mind, to explore the highway of the soul. Approach the unknown with respect, high ideals, and trust in God.

D. Origins of Your Patterns

You may ask, "How can I learn from my past if I don't remember it?" Or, "How can I learn from my mistakes if I don't recall them?" Good questions. We could just as easily ask, "How are you linked to your ancestors even though you don't remember them?" Or, "Where do our instincts come from?" Those questions could continue, but to what advantage? Those who accept the continuity of life need no further proof. Skeptics will continue to live by their codes of skepticism. Each is entitled to his or her own reality system.

The reality of past lives is not the most important question; the *application* of what is learned from the subconscious is of primary importance. How can this study help us to become happier, healthier and wiser individuals? How can this research lead us to the realization of our unconscious patterns, our talents or our shortcomings?

For myself, the work with past lives has been the most productive work over a lifetime. I cannot predict what it will or will not bring to you. If you acknowledge and appreciate whatever you are given – whether a little or a lot – then you open the door to more. For some people, the inner mind gives only a little at first, almost as a test to see what they will do with that information. In subsequent sessions, more and more is given.

With a few sessions completed, major patterns will begin to surface or will come to light. You will soon recognize those patterns as habits or beliefs from deep within yourself. Regressions are like spiritual evaluation sessions. They allow you to chart or to measure your progress in the Earth School continuing educational program.

E. Remembering Who You Are

Assuming that you have completed the chapters on IDEALS and EMBRACING YOUR ETERNAL CHILD, and have used your tapes, you are now ready for your third Inner Adventure – THE SOUL'S REMEMBRANCES. Here is an inner adventure that can bring fuller understanding of your higher self; the *You* that encompasses numerous lives and countless experiences.

The adventure progresses – there is a quickening and a feeling of excitement each time we take the sacred journey, deep within, to our stored memories. This is not a journey over distance or time, but a journey through the dimensions of your being. The pathway is TRUST, the purpose is forgiveness and enlightenment.

Regressions respond to the rhythmic beat of your ancient heart – they are the true "roots" of your deeper self. Progressions are the fruits of your tomorrows – even though those fruits are still buds. Progressions are the history of your future. They are your road to spiritual recovery: A HEALING JOURNEY.

F. Remembering the Future

Throughout history, people have been fascinated, tantalized, and awed by life's greatest mystery: death. The inevitability of death and fear of its unknown aftermath bring apprehension and dread to many. What happens when one dies? What becomes of one's identity, one's personality, one's ego, when the transition is made to the state of death? Many people fear that at death their identities will be annihilated and that their consciousness of being a unique individual will be lost forever. This mystery and the concerns that it causes have prompted virtually every civilization – from the ancient Egyptians and the early Eastern religions to those of modern times – to try to answer this question, hoping to provide comfort and reassurance to their followers.

Most religions teach that there is an existence after death, but not all agree on its form. Since there is no way to prove (or disprove) their teachings, belief has always been a matter of faith. In modern times, however, in spite of skepticism, and even hostility in some cases, several enlightened researchers have been making efforts to unravel this mystery and have had encouraging results. There are many documented cases which suggest that individuals have re-entered the physical world with memories of a past life. There are also thousands of documented cases of what is known as a "Near Death Experience," in which people have been pronounced "clinically dead," but then returned to their bodies reporting startlingly similar experiences, all suggesting that there is an existence beyond the material plane.

What can we do to improve our lives and to prepare better for the death experience and the life beyond? Hospice is a highly respected international organization of professionals and volunteers who assist people through the process of dying. In my training to be a hospice volunteer, I was taught that most of us wait until our final days to evaluate our lives. Sadly, at that stage it is too late to make any changes.

Thanks to Dr. Milton H. Erickson, along with other pioneers and innovators in healing and hypnosis, people can now evaluate their lives while there is still time to do something constructive.

During the next guided exercise a safe, spiritual environment is created for maximum accomplishment. The exercise will take you on an extraordinary journey of discovery and enlightenment. It begins with a review of short-term present life events, and then proceeds to explore long-term, past-life memories. The past and present are assimilated through a dialogue for application and betterment. You are then guided safely to pre-view the future of your present life. Future insights or prophesies are "probabilities," or "possibilities," based upon your current ideals and directions. Future potentials can always be changed by your actions, decisions, and free will.

You also can choose to envision the events and circumstances that lead to your death, and even rise above the death experience itself. From this unique perspective, you honestly and wisely can evaluate the gains and losses of this lifetime.

Objectively studying your death experiences (both past-life and present-life future) allays any fear of death and teaches the "continuity of life." Self-hypnosis, used spiritually, is one of the safest approaches to soul exploration – past, present, and future. This is an enriching adventure of self-discovery and spiritual purpose.

The following 14 steps will help you to understand the regression and progression procedure. Then, make your tape. You'll need an hour length tape, or a tape that has 60 minutes on one side. Use your tape only about once a month, as you need ample time to assimilate the meaning and lessons of each session.

G. Accessing the Soul's Remembrances

1. Inner Adventure — Procedure

This Inner Adventure begins with Age Regression exercises from your current life. Then you will proceed to a past-life that is pertinent and meaningful to your current work with Patterns. You will analyze the Soul Lessons and then complete the Forgiveness exercises.

Next you can explore present life in the future. If you wish to continue, you may progress to the death experience, not in a macabre manner, but as a healing and helpful exercise.

There are 14 basic steps in past-life exploration sessions. The depth level of self-hypnosis varies with each individual, as does the pace and timing. Everyone responds with his or her own temperament, style, and experience.

Here are the steps.

Each step flows naturally into the next:

1. *Self-Hypnosis* — entering your own relaxed, receptive, 100% natural level of mind. This experience

belongs to YOU. You do the real work. You are in control. You accept or reject anything you wish.

Begin with progressive relaxation, relaxing first the head, then the rest of your body in sequence, working to the toes. This method first relaxes the head and mind – the rest of the body follows easily. As you count down, you easily reach your natural level of relaxation. This is the Alpha state; there is no hurry, so don't rush.

2. *Present-life Regression* — you recall or process pleasant memories from your life, if possible. A few individuals have no pleasant memories. In this case one could recall youthful memories of family, friends, or of going to school.

There are two common types of recall: detached and total immersion. To illustrate each, you might recall stubbing a toe. In detachment you might say, "I remember that I stubbed my toe." In immersion you exclaim, "Ouch! I stubbed my toe!" – you relive the event.

Detached narrative is more frequent. Some people respond in both detached and immersed modes as they process information.

3. *Prenatal Regression* — you recall the time just before birth.

4. *Blue Mist Experience* — here you experience the dimension between your current life and a previous life. Many perceive it as a "blue mist," others as a light of varying shades, yet others as a mist of different colors. Any way you perceive it is correct for you. Most

people experience peace, detachment and timeless-ness; a timeless place in a place-less time.

You may bring all things to your remembrance as you journey upon the "avenue of the heart." This is a spiritual exercise, not an intellectual one. You'll find much satisfaction and accomplishment in working with your emotional and spiritual memory.

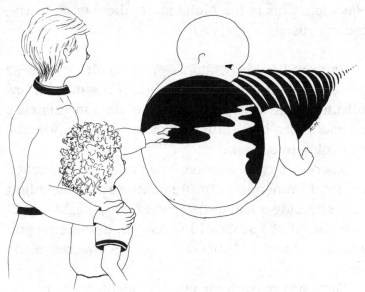

BLUE MIST — TUNNEL OF TIME
Artist: Kathye Mendes

5.   *Entering the Past Life* — with your eyes closed, you mentally look down at your feet and note what you are wearing there, if anything. If you perceive several kinds of footwear, you may be trying to process several lives – choose one.

If your perceptions are predominantly visual in that life, you'll SEE your feet. If more kinesthetic, you'll FEEL what's on your feet. If you're more auditory, you'll HEAR inner promptings or information.

Going slowly up the body, "What are you wearing? How does it look? How does it feel?"

6. *Processing the Life* — TRUST what you are now given, what you receive or perceive. Let the story tell itself; just "step aside" and allow the information to come in its own way, at its own pace.

There is no foretelling what life you will relive, nor your race, religion, gender, or personality. Each person has had many lives and has been different characters in each of them. Some have been notable and some notorious. Most were as ordinary as we are in our present life. Specific dates, places, and names are not as important as the major events of a life. More feeling and emotion are associated with significant events than with details of time, place or "coins of the realm."

Simple open-ended questions prompt a wealth of information and clear memory. i.e. "What happens next?" "What's going on now?" "What are you doing?"

7. *Death Experience* — a safe and positive way to complete the life's memory. You detach from any physical pain or discomfort and view the actual death with calm and detachment. You may respond with curiosity and interest as you look down upon your lifeless face and body. Now comes a realization of spiritual immortality.

Some souls seem to linger for awhile without knowing quite where to go or what to. Some go to a light, others have departed friends or family waiting for them. Some reported that after just a few days the lifetime started to seem as if it were just a dream. One woman drifted to her far-off childhood home, hoping to resolve childhood conflicts with her brother. Her spirit was seen by the brother, but he could not hear her.

8. *Soul Lessons* — the lessons learned from your deep past are *the most important* reasons for this work. The reasons for a life may be unclear, but the lessons and patterns profound. You may discover talents and values you have not recognized or appreciated. Many find reservoirs of generosity, patience, service or other qualities for which they rarely give themselves credit. They come away with knowledge that builds understanding and self-esteem. Names and dates are only the bones of the past; soul lessons are the lasting gift of life.

9. *Forgiveness* — release anger and grief, allow spiritual and emotional traumas to heal with those exercises. This is a time to experience love and gratitude for past-life relationships with friends and lovers. Especially forgive those who have hurt you, or that you have hurt.

Mentally look into the eyes of each person from that life and send love and forgiveness. You bless them, release them and let them fade.

Take plenty of time for this important step, there is no rush. You may hold an inner dialogue to integrate past-life self with present-life self. Some people desire to give themselves a specific activity or task to help in forgiveness of self or of others. Any way you wish to do this is correct for you, as you are guided by your ideals and higher wisdom.

10. *Return through Blue Mist* — bringing back with you something special, a gift, a lesson learned, or a positive pattern realized.

11. *Protective Suggestions* — you retain in your conscious mind only that which is important, helpful, and beneficial. On rare occasions someone may choose to pass through a "veil of forgetfulness" and not bring back any conscious memory of the life.

12. *Return to Present – Onward to Future* — returning to current time and place; or, you may progress ahead in time. It is possible to gain valuable foresight in processing the present-life future, even evaluating the present life from the perspective of going beyond its completion. Patterns, lessons, and opportunities of the current life are examined. Future progression exercise is optional, included only if you wish to do it.

13. *Wake-up Procedure* — suggestions for total normalization, adapted to your own pace and well-being.

14. *Discussion and Evaluation of Session* – you were encouraged not to evaluate the information as it unfolds, but rather to save all self-analysis for discussion after the session. Treasure the gifts you were given from your deep memory; discuss your experience with close friends or loved ones.

In discussing the information, you may find that the door to your memory is still open. It is possible that more material from the past life may come to light at this time. For some, the door remains open for days or weeks. They may dream or daydream about the life. Keep a diary or journal of those memories for further insight and understanding.

If you fell asleep during the session, learn from that mistake. Next time, use your most energetic part of the day to do this important work, even to the point of sitting up or kneeling in an uncomfortable position.

With time and patience, as you study your past-life lessons, you can analyze your patterns and help solve problems in your current life. Each regression session is a sacred experience — a true vision quest. The experience is uniquely personal and different for everyone. Evaluate the learning for yourself by using the "Personal Evaluation and Self-Study Sheets" at the end of this chapter. Then, and only then, should you accept the validity of your own experience. Most of all, ENJOY your adventures through time, and experience the sheer JOY of discovery.

After you experience your regression sessions, whether guided by self or another, you can begin the process of synthesis:

(a)   First you observed the session or felt it or heard or perceived information and experiences and feelings.

(b)   Now, you transcribe the information into a journal, diary, or onto the appropriate sheet at the end of this chapter, entitled, "Analyzing the Life." Who were the people, what did they do, what did you do, when — in time — was the general era of your experience, where was the location, what did you learn, what was the lesson, and whom did you forgive?

(c) Now you define and compare the information. Evaluate if or how it applies to your current life.

(d) If possible, you might investigate that specific era of history. Check your library for historical materials; what other books do they have related to that time or place?

(e) Finally, decide how you feel about the life itself. Do you recognize it inside you? Is it plausible, or even probable? What can you do to use this memory in your current life?

The time that you use now to apply those vital steps will be well spent. This is an exceedingly worthwhile time, rich and valuable. You will notice the evidence of this in the positive results harvested in the months and years to come.

Also, feel free to talk. Share your memories and experiences with trusted and loving friends. Avoid discussing past-life memories with skeptics and disbelievers; you will find this an exercise in frustration. Share only with your dearest and most positive friends.

2. Inner Adventure — Exercise

(Read at about 1/3 your normal pace)

Before we start, make yourself comfortable in a place where you can relax without being disturbed for about an hour.

Now that you are ready, just look forward or upward; you don't need to look at anything specific. I am going to count down slowly from ten to one. With every descending number, you can just slowly blink your eyes, as if in slow motion, with every number.

Ten, that's good, do it nice and slowly.

Nine, that's good

Eight (2 second pause)

Seven (2 second pause)

Six (2 second pause)

Five (2 second pause)

Four (2 second pause

Three (2 second pause)

Two (2 second pause)

One.

Now you can just close your eyes, and I will tell you what that was for and why we did it. We are going to do an exercise called progressive relaxation, where we simply relax the different parts of your body sequentially. That was just to relax your eyelids. Right now, isn't there a feeling of relaxation, or a comfortable tired feeling in your eyelids? Whatever the feeling is, just allow that to multiply, to magnify, and to become greater. This is something that you do; nobody else can do it for you. So just take your time, and don't be concerned if there is any little movement in your eyelids. That is called REM, or rapid eye movement, and it is a perfectly natural part of this experience.

Now, just allow that feeling of relaxation to move outward, as in imaginary waves or ripples, to the entire facial area. Just think about relaxing the face. Feel the relaxation going on outward to the entire head area, relaxing the head. Now let the relaxation flow down to your neck, to your shoulders, down the arms and into the hands, relaxing that entire area.

Take a deep breath and fill your lungs with relaxation, and allow that relaxation to flow to the solar plexus, to the spine, slowly down your spine to the hips, to the legs, the feet, and all the way out to your toes, filling your entire body with relaxation. Now, just slow down a little bit and mentally examine your entire body. If there is any area that is not completely relaxed, just allow that part to catch up and to become as relaxed as the rest.

(Pause a few seconds)

Now allow yourself to slow down just a little bit more, then a bit more, and I am going to count downward once again from ten to one. This time, with every descending number, just allow yourself to slow down, becoming more still, more centered, with every number, and at the count of one, you can enter your own natural level of relaxation. I will count more rapidly now – ten, nine, eight, seven, six, five, four, three, two, one.

You are now at your own natural level of relaxation, and from this level you may move to any other level with complete awareness and may function at will, because you are in complete control at every level of your mind. This is something that you want. It is here and it is now.

(pause a few seconds)

Now let us begin by comparing your mind to the surface of a quiet pond. On the surface everything looks peaceful and still, but below the surface there is great depth and much is happening. You can think of my voice as a breeze whispering in the trees along the shore.

(Pause briefly)

Not everyone realizes his or her full capacities, and you have to discover those capacities in whatever way you wish. One of the things I would like for you to discover is that your own subconscious mind can listen to me and also deal with something at the same time. Perhaps you can remember doing this as a child in school, gazing out the window while the teacher was talking. (Pause) Or, walking with a friend and talking to that friend at the same time. Two separate things, yet happening at the same time. Your subconscious is *here* and can hear every word, so you don't have to think or to move about or to make any sort of effort. You are in a place where you can let go safely, and just relax.

You may take a deep breath now, and you will notice that a drifting might occur. You may feel light, you may feel heavy, or you may feel that your body is asleep, although your mind is alert. There is less and less importance to be attached to my voice, and more and more significance to be given to your own inner reality, to your own inner experience. Stored deep in your subconscious are wonderful memories of other times and other places. Your subconscious can call upon and access those memories, memories you only thought you had misplaced. Experiences that you only thought you had mislaid. In due time, in your own time, your subconscious will reveal those memories to you in a dream, or a daydream, or sometime when you are not especially thinking about it. You may experience those memories of other times and other places.

By looking deeply into the recesses of your mind, you can see your vision and hear the voice of your heart. With this insight, comes new growth and new understanding. Later you can apply this knowledge to understand yourself and the world better. In a moment now, we can begin a series of exercises that will lead into memory recall and future possibilities.

You may begin by moving yourself backward in time, going back now to a time when you are about 15 years old. You are about 15 years old now. Choose a pleasant, happy memory of that time, if possible. You will find it is very easy for you to do this. Choose one specific memory or one specific event you wish to process from the time you were about 15. Note what is happening. (Pause) What are you doing? What do you see or feel?

I will be quiet now to give you ample time to enjoy this event. You may hear voices, you may see or sense other people. The images may be in vivid color as in a cinema movie, or they may be black and white, or only vague outlines. You may hear memories whispered in your inner ear, or you may only sense the memory. It really doesn't matter how you perceive the memory, just let it happen. You are about 15 years old now. What is happening?

(45 second pause)

Now take this memory with you as you continue to move backward to the time you are about four or five years old. Again, choose a pleasant, happy memory, an impression, an episode, an experience in your life, then focus on this memory, look at it clearly. See what you are wearing; become aware of any people around you. Look and listen to what is going on. Reach down deeply and feel it. You are now four or five years old. What are you doing? (Pause) What do you see or feel, or even hear, as you are about four or five? Again I will be quiet while you process this experience.

(45 second pause)

Take this memory with you also as you continue going back, very quickly, through the years of three, two, and one, moving on through the time of your birth and going to that very safe, warm, and secure place where nothing can harm you. A place where you feel surrounded, protected, and loved. This is a good place, a place of forming and growth. (Pause)

Now you find that you can go on beyond this, going into the Blue Mist; the Blue Mist surrounds you and protects you. The Blue Mist is a time of inner peace, of quiet movement, of gentle sounds and easy rhythms. It is a time of renewal, and a time of great patience. The Blue Mist is a time without measurement, a place without distance or boundaries: a timeless place in a place-less time.

The Blue Mist is really the avenue from the heart to the infinite. But even though you are so very comfortable and happy here, a part of you longs for something more. A part of you longs for activity and experience, and this longing grows to become a great desire. This desire guides you to look toward the horizon, or as if you were looking through a long tunnel, or walking down a long corridor. You perceive a light. You realize that the light is good, so you begin going, growing toward the light.

You travel toward the light, not on the pathway of the head or the intellect, but on the pathway of the heart and feelings. For through the avenue of the heart, all things are revealed to you. Soon you come into the light. The light comes in through the top of your head and fills your entire being with light. The light heals you, it surrounds you and protects you, and you feel the life energies throughout your entire being.

You take a deep breath now. You go beyond the Blue Mist and find yourself at a still earlier time. You look downward and place your feet firmly on the earth in fullness of strength. This happens quite automatically, without any effort or forethought on your part. Simply allow it to happen.

As you step firmly onto the earth in fullness of strength, mentally look down and note what you are wearing on your feet. What do you perceive on your feet? (Pause one minute) Going slowly up your body, note what you are wearing. How does it look or feel? Feel the texture, see the colors. (One minute pause) TRUST the impressions that you receive, even though it might seem like imagination, at first.

Do you have anything on your head? (Pause) Do you have anything in your hands? (Pause) Are you male or female? (Pause) What are you doing? How do you feel? Let the story tell itself.

(Pause for one minute)

Now in your mind's eye, slowly look around the place where you are standing, and make a mental note of what you see. Look around and note what you perceive. Again, I will be quiet while you make a complete turn, looking in all directions about you, making a note of the important things that you see. Process the information and record it so you can bring it back later.

(Pause one minute).

Note your home or dwelling place. (one minute).

And now, you may look for other people, or a time when you feel yourself near or with other people. Make a note of the people, your impressions, and feelings. Perhaps there is someone special, someone with whom you have a close bond, an affinity, or a strong connection.

(Pause one minute)

Now look for some vehicle of transportation, something you might have ridden on or in, something that feels familiar when you sit in or on it. Or note anything that others are using for transportation. Make a note of the methods of transportation.

(Pause one minute)

At this time you might also wish to taste something that you are eating. What are you eating? Can you smell the food cooking? Can you taste it? Make a note of this and record the information.

(Pause one minute)

Now, if you listen carefully, you may hear your own name being spoken by a friend or someone calling out to you. What do they call you? What is your work or profession? What are you learning?

(Pause one minute)

As you look for clues, can you tell what land this is? Perhaps you can perceive what century or what period this is. Record this information. (Pause)

Now move to the time of an important event in your life, a significant episode. Note what is happening. (Pause) What do you see or feel? (Pause) Do you hear any sounds, or notice any smells? (Pause one minute) Move now to the next important event or another significant time in that life. What is happening now? (Pause) What are you doing? (Pause one minute)

You may move now to the event and circumstances that lead to your death, and to the death experience itself. Detach yourself from any physical pain or discomfort but note the events and the death experience, itself. (Pause one minute) As you pass from that life, you may float safely and gently above your body and above the life, going to that timeless place and placeless time where all things are revealed clearly in all their fullness.

From this higher perspective, what were the lessons you learned from this life? (Pause) How did you grow? (Pause) What could you have done better? (Pause) What brought you the greatest happiness or fulfillment in the life? (Pause) What caused the most sadness or hurt? (Pause) What did you learn or accomplish in that life that can help you in your present life? (Pause)

In light of those new discoveries and understanding, please relay a message from your past-life self to your present-life self. What does your past-life self wish to communicate to the present-life self? (Pause) In return, give a message from your present-life self to your past-life self. (Pause) What does the present You say to that part of your past? (Pause)

What task or activity could you perform in your current life that would help to heal and to balance that life? (Pause one minute)

Now look into the eyes of that past-life self from your present eyes and send your blessings, your love, and your compassion. (Pause) Bless that part of you and let it fade. Look also into the eyes of everyone you saw, those you have loved, that person who was special to you, and send love. And as you do this important step, as you bless them and send them your love, release them, let them fade. As they fade, let them go as they bless and forgive you. Let the veil slowly drop. Allow the curtain to close slowly. Allow a full healing of that life and that time. (Pause one minute)

Now as you prepare for the journey back, you will bring back with you only that which is helpful and beneficial for you in this life. Bring back something holy or special – a gem of wisdom, but only what you want. You may release other feelings, memories, or impressions now, and retain in your conscious mind only that which is important, helpful, and beneficial for you to retain at this time.

Now slowly you return through the Blue Mist, traveling on the avenue of the heart, where all things are revealed to you through that warm and safe place where nothing can harm you – returning through the levels of your mind and bringing back the information that you have recorded. Slowly come back through the years into what we call the present life.

Now move forward in time to the year 2005. What is happening now? (Pause) What do you see? What do you feel? What is going on in 2005? (Pause) Now move forward to the year 2010. It is now 2010, trust the impressions. What are you doing? (Pause) What is happening?

(Pause) Move on forward to the time of an important event in your life beyond 2010. What are you doing? (Pause) What is happening? (Pause one minute)

The final exercise is optional, only if you wish to do it. You have full understanding and realization that death is merely the next step in every life. With this understanding, if you wish, you may move to the events and circumstances leading to your death. What are the events and circumstances that lead to your death and the death experience? (Pause one minute) now as you review your present life from beyond death, what was a pattern or lesson of this life? (Pause 30 seconds) How did you gain or grow in this life? (Pause 30 seconds) How did you lose, or what could you have done better? (Pause 30 seconds) What brought you the greatest happiness or fulfillment? (Pause 30 seconds) What caused you the most sadness or hurt? (Pause 30 seconds) What were your greatest strengths – what worked well? (Pause 30 seconds)

Remember this information so that you may bring it back with you in order that it may be of help and betterment in your eternal journey, in your evolution through time and timeless time.

It is now time for you to return to what we call the present time, this day and this place. As you return, realize that you have done very well. You have opened in trust and thankfulness. In a little while, I will count from one to ten. As I count, reorient yourself fully into the present, and at the count of ten you will be wide awake, refreshed, feeling better than before.

I will count very slowly:

One, stepping firmly and fully into the present.

Two, feel total normalization at every level of your being.

Three, feel the life energies returning to your extremities.

Four, you may wish to move your hands, feet, or neck.

Five

Six

Seven, coming up to your full potential.

Eight, reenergizing.

Nine, Revitalized, and

Ten, slowly open your eyes. You are wide awake, wide awake. Welcome back!

Now it's time to synthesize the information you received. Gather your subconscious memories and put them into written form. The process of writing them will help to open even more impressions and feelings, and it will sharpen your recall. You could draw or sketch scenes or objects that you saw.

Later you can evaluate that information and can begin the process of slowly and wisely changing your behaviors. Changing behaviors will change patterns. Take realistic steps, proceeding from a place of strength based upon your new-found knowledge and guided by your ideals.

H. Personal Evaluation

1. Self-Study Sheets

Note: Use extra paper, or you may list questions and your answers in a personal journal.

1. Session date. Who guided this session?

2. Write a little about your present-life memories processed in the session.

3. How did you perceive the "Blue Mist" or the time between lives?

4. What did you have on your feet? What clothing were you wearing?

5. Describe your home or dwelling place.

6. Who were the people involved in the life?

7. What was a major event in your life?

8. Another significant event?

9. What was a method of transportation?

10. What was your occupation or activity?

11. Describe the circumstances leading to your death, and the death experience itself.

12. What happened after you died?

13. What were the most important lessons from that life?

14. What talents or abilities did you refine or develop?

15. What made you the happiest or gave the greatest fulfillment in the life?

16. What caused the most sadness or hurt?

17. What could you have done better?

18. Did you visually bless the other people in the life and forgive them?

19. Did you hold an inner dialogue with aspects of your eternal self?

20. Did you give yourself a forgiveness task? If so, explain.

21. Which pattern(s) were you working with in the life? What were the origins or "root causes?"

22. It is not crucial, but interesting, to see if you can recall a probable time frame and geographical area of the life lived.

23. Were there any people in that life whom you recognize in your current life? What were their roles then, and now?

24. Was this life one that you had knowledge of before the session?

25. Were you able to apply the lessons and patterns of that life to your present circumstances?

26. Is there anything you would like to write or sketch about the future?

2. Analyzing the Life: Story Frame

Synopsis of the life (briefly explain the life):

How did you *gain* or *grow* in that life?

How did you *lose*, or what could you have *done better*?

What can you bring back from that life that will help you in your current life?

What are your opportunities for *forgiveness*?

What specific tasks can you carry out in your current life that will help to *heal* or to *balance* the memory?

Which recurrent themes or patterns reflect in your current life?

CHAPTER VIII

Soul Lessons —
Edgar and Gertrude Cayce

A. Edgar and Gertrude Cayce

"Who and what is thy pattern?" (Edgar Cayce reading 357-13)

O f all the people who have been instrumental in the study and application of patterns and soul lessons, Edgar Cayce is outstanding. Mr. Cayce's story is so amazing that no single biography can explain the full scope of his life and his work. It is probable that if you were to read every available book about him you would begin to gain only an inkling of how important his work is, and how it will continue to illuminate the lives of countless future generations. (There are over three hundred books *about* Edgar Cayce and his work, but he wrote none of them himself!)

With no medical training and little formal schooling, Edgar Cayce, while in self-hypnosis, astounded doctors with his holistic healing techniques and perplexed scholars with his pioneering work in the highest realms of Mind. He diagnosed medical problems

1903

EDGAR AND GERTRUDE CAYCE.
HE BOLDLY TRAVELED WHERE FEW HAVE
DARED TO VENTURE

Artist: Julia Fierman

and prescribed remedies while in trance. He was able to do this without seeing, or even knowing, the individuals concerned. While in trance, he needed only to be given the name and address of a particular individual, and would give a discourse (called a reading) on the condition of that person. Not only was he able to describe with great accuracy the physical condition of the person's body, he was able while in this state to look into the future and the past, in many cases relating present physical ailments to events which had occurred in past lives.

Edgar Cayce was born in 1877 in Kentucky and spent his boyhood years on the family farm, where the fresh air and open spaces agreed with him. He developed a strong interest in the Bible while still a child, and in his preteens resolved to read it completely through once every year for his entire life. He had a strong Christian faith and drew on the inspiration and guidance he found in the Scriptures, along with prayer, to aid him in discovering and in attuning himself to God's will.

In his youth, Cayce's life was a simple one, typical of that of most boys of his generation. Occasionally, however, his unusual psychic gifts became manifest. For example, one day, while he was alone in the woods and reading the Bible, an angel appeared to him in a vision, told him that his prayers had been answered, and asked him what he desired. He replied that he wanted to be able to help people, especially children. This desire to help others was the driving force in Cayce's life, and, when giving readings, his primary concern was that the information be accurate and beneficial to the people for whom they were given.

Edgar Cayce's special healing gifts were used first on himself. At the age of fifteen, while playing ball at school, he was struck in the spine by a ball. The blow left him acting strangely for the rest of the day. That night, after having gone to bed, in a trance-like state he told his parents what had happened and what to do to correct the problem. They complied and the next morning he was normal, having no recollection of anything that had occurred since he had been struck.

In his early twenties, Cayce lost the use of his voice; for over a year he was able to converse only in a whisper. Local medical doctors were unable to help him. A traveling stage hypnotist was able, through hypnotic suggestion, to give some relief, but it was only temporary. Eventually a local man, who had taken correspondence courses in hypnosis and osteopathy, guided him into trance. While in trance, he described the cause of his problem, and explained in a normal tone of voice that it could be corrected through certain specific suggestions. The recommended suggestions were made, and when he awakened, Cayce's voice was normal. He remembered nothing that had taken place while in trance.

This experience led him in 1901 to begin giving readings for other people. He continued those readings, typically twice a day, for the next 43 years, until his death in 1945. The complete significance of his work is yet to be appreciated to the full extent. Even so, he is now recognized as one of the most amazing men of the twentieth century. And this was a man who was initially very reluctant to use his exceptional ability.

Cayce's intuitive healing of his own injury opened

the door that led him to be a guiding light and an incredible channel of healing for others. Of the millions who are familiar with Edgar's work, few know the vital role that his wife played. Gertrude Cayce was born February 22, 1880, and died within a few months of her husband on Easter Sunday, 1945. She is revered and remembered by those who knew her for her absolute integrity and dependability.

Gertrude Cayce was a devoted wife and mother, as well as the strength behind Edgar's work. He would never have achieved what he did were it not for this remarkable woman. She carefully avoided the glare of publicity and drew no attention to herself. During the forty three years that Cayce gave readings, she guided most of them; her job-description was "Conductor."

As conductor, she saw to it that he was comfortable and made certain that no one touched his body or passed anything over it while he was in trance. Edgar was totally open to suggestions at this time, and it was Gertrude's responsibility to review the questions that individuals had submitted in writing, and to read them to Cayce at the proper time. Gertrude's working title has changed today, but the responsibility of such work remains the same. Rather than "conductor," today she would be called a "guide" or a "facilitator."

In the early days of Cayce's work, the position Gertrude later assumed was abused by various conductors who would tag on questions at the end of a session, asking for tips on such trivialities as horse races or other competitive sports. Unscrupulous doctors inserted long needles into Cayce's entranced body to see if he faked trance. Edgar was not aware of anything while in this hypnotic state, and he began to

emerge from it with terrible headaches. Those headaches became even worse, and when Cayce learned of
the ridiculous requests being appended to his sessions, he abandoned the work and moved to Selma,
Alabama.

In Selma, he opened a photography studio. When
one of his sons, Hugh Lynn, suffered a bad burn and,
temporarily, was blinded, he turned again to the readings. He trusted only Gertrude now, and when they
realized what a good team they were, he decided once
again to give readings for other people.

The Cayces' last living son, Edgar Evans Cayce,
revealed a part of their story to me in a personal in-
terview. Edgar Evans Cayce related how patient and
accepting his mother was, and that, after Cayce's bad
experiences with other conductors, his mother became
the sole conductor for her husband.

Mrs. Cayce always screened people's questions.
Only inquiries of the highest and purest nature were
allowed. Gertrude obtained more than seventy of her
husband's readings for herself, the earliest involving
her search for the cure of her tuberculosis, followed by
readings of dream interpretation, the clearing of skin
rashes and eye problems, and once a reading for healing following a serious fall down a flight of stairs.
Edgar and Gertrude Cayce's lives were a tender love
story of trust, integrity, and faith utilized to make
manifest the love of God and man.

Gertrude was expert at making do with little, and
many times they lived in extreme poverty. But
Gertrude had a strong character, loved her children
and husband deeply, and devoted herself to keeping
the family together.

Edgar Cayce now had a conductor in whom he could trust implicitly, he grew and evolved into a dynamic and powerful channel. And yet, there was something missing – the necessary stenographer, for at that time tape recorders were unknown. A young woman was hired who quickly became a part of the family. Gladys Davis and Gertrude took an immediate liking to one another and remained lifelong friends, both of them dedicated to Edgar and his work. Subsequent life readings explained their previous connection in past lives. Now the team was complete: channel, conductor, and stenographer. Together they made a strong, harmonious working unit, and for many years their work was a beacon of light to humanity, especially throughout the dark years of World War II. Gertrude remained the unsung heroine of Cayce's work, humble and quiet in her perseverance and support.

The Cayce readings point out that Edgar Cayce's abilities were not unique to him, that we all have the potential to accomplish what he did. There were apparently two sources that he accessed to obtain his information. The first is the subconscious minds of all humans are interconnected, and what is known to one is accessible to all. The second source was described as the superconscious mind, or the level of mind at which each individual soul is aware of its relationship to God, the source of all knowledge and wisdom. Attunement to the superconscious makes this source of infinite knowledge available to all.

Cayce tells us that, at the superconscious level, we can gain access to the Akashic Record, a chronicle of everything that has ever been thought, said, or done by everyone who has ever lived. The Akashic Record, also referred to in the readings as the Book of Life, or the Book of God's Remembrance, can be thought of as the revelation of the Creator's all-encompassing wisdom and knowledge. According to the Cayce readings, contact with both the subconscious and the superconscious is possible for all minds, making the infinite wisdom of the superconscious available to each one of us.

To communicate with those levels of consciousness, we need the ability to put our egos aside and attune ourselves to God, the universal source. In Edgar Cayce, this ability was developed much more highly than it is in most people (the readings attribute this to his many lifetimes as a healer), but the sources that he drew upon and the information he obtained are available to everyone.

Edgar Cayce's greatest contribution to mankind is the collection of 14,306 transcribed readings which spanned a time period of over 40 years (1901 – 1944). They are now available for research and study at the library of the Association for Research and Enlightenment at Virginia Beach, Virginia, where they are indexed under more than ten thousand major subject headings. The readings began as physical, or health, readings, but eventually expanded in scope to encompass the range of spiritual awareness. Most of the readings were for individuals, and thus deal with specific personal questions regarding physical, mental, vocational, and spiritual life. Some of them, however, are discourses on topics such as reincarnation, Bible interpretation, ancient civilizations, world affairs, and others.

They teach that there is a oneness of all force, and that force is God. God is Light, Life, and Love. Humans, all of us, are spiritual beings, children of God, with a continuity of life that has existed and will exist throughout eternity. The sojourn in the Earth plane embraces the concepts of reincarnation, balance, and grace. The readings tell us that all questions can be answered if we but seek the Spirit within, listen to what the Spirit tells us, and trust that Spirit for the proper information, guidance, and healing. So while Cayce is remembered primarily for contributions as a healer, his philosophy extends to our entire physical and spiritual lives.

Cayce's readings emphasize that we are spiritual beings, and that all healing comes from within; the body contains the wisdom to heal itself, and will do so when given the environment and the opportunity. What is the source of this healing? The readings state that the body's innate ability to heal itself is the direct result of the manifestation of the Divine Spirit within it. This assertion makes sense when we consider that healing is a universal property of all creation, and takes place constantly and naturally in nature.

Cayce's readings stress that a proper motivation and the establishment of a spiritual ideal are most important in our lives. The readings tell us that we can understand our bodies best in terms of three-dimensional concepts, reflecting a three-dimensional world in which we live. We have a physical body, a mental body, and a spiritual body. Each is a separate part of us; yet, they are one and the same. The Cayce readings compare the relationship of those three bodies to that of the Christian Holy Trinity – Father, Son, and

Days Of Our Past Lives
Artist: Veronica Reed

the Holy Spirit. Scientists are also recognizing that no line can be drawn between psyche and soma, between mind and body.

Cayce's work touched upon the soul in all its varied aspects, and in the entire body of Cayce's work, those readings pertaining to how souls gained or lost are the most insightful and helpful in our study of patterns. Edgar often counseled that individuals pattern their lives after the Master, Jesus. He was a great advocate that people should access *their own* inner guidance and information, referring to: "...that may be obtained from their own subconscious...." (Reading #254-46) He advocated numerous methods for recalling past lives, but often reminded people to maintain a balanced purpose and to keep their ideals clear throughout such a search, and not to become side-tracked or begin to abuse the gift of recall.

Among Cayce's practical methods for recall was the active use of the imagination: that is the image storage and retrieval faculty of the mind – *not* an imaginative warehouse of fantasy resembling a Disney movie. Cayce told how visual images and even odors would hearken back to past-life memories, and how most of our deepest fears have their roots in the distant past.

Cayce often advocated the study of various periods of history which were of particular interest to a person. Where would this interest originate if not from one's heredity or past memories? The study of scenery and painting can be used to open memories, as well as the sight of certain monuments. Drumming, chanting, or music may stir feelings or echoes of ancient memory. The slightest recognition of past familiarity may be an avenue to past recall.

B. An Excellent Adventure

One of Cayce's most popular methods advocated the use of travel. He instructed some people to travel to specific sites and locations in order to open their deep memories. Children often experienced spontaneous recall triggered by an event or an artifact from history. Some subconsciously named dolls or pets with a name used in a past life.

Dreams and meditation were major sources recommended for past-life recall. Also, physical stimulation such as massage could trigger past memories buried deeply in the muscle and bone. All of those methods may be used to gain an understanding of how the past can heal the present.

In addition, the reuniting of loved ones and the subsequent recall of past-life relationships may rekindle the experience of love in a former life. Love, sexuality, and spirituality all are linked to our past lives. (Those topics will be discussed at length in a later chapter). In some cases, Mr. Cayce's readings counseled people *not* to attempt the recall of certain lives or particular memories. His word of warning to one individual was: "As to the experiences in the earth, these have been many and quite varied. Many of these are not well even to be known to self, and thus have they been blotted from the book of thy remembrance..." (Reading #5231-1) Cayce often counseled that where there is a past, leave it behind, and begin where you are today.

What Cayce's source *did* advocate, and often, was to minimize the faults and magnify the virtues found in each past and present life. This should be the purpose and practice of each individual entity.

This study of how souls gained and lost in previous lives might easily constitute a book unto itself. For an introductory understanding, we shall touch briefly upon this aspect of Cayce's material. Should your interest be aroused, then, you may go straight to the "source" for further study.

C. How Souls Lost

Let us consider the issue of how souls may have lost. There are about 350 life readings discussing how persons lost in previous lives. The following list is not comprehensive, as it was compiled before the computer ROM disk was available; but it is still valuable in giving us the direction and focus of the Cayce perspective. This list was compiled a few years ago and is available at the A.R.E. Library under the heading, "Soul Retrogression."

I have listed twenty-four categories in alphabetical order:

How souls lost:
1. Anger (15 people)
2. Condemnation (37 ")
3. Contention (14")
4. Disappointment (8 ")
5. Fear (21 ")
6. Grudges and hatred (66 ")
7. Materiality (67 ")
8. Misapplication (24 ")
9. Oppression and overbearance (19 ")
10. Persecution and prejudice (5 ")
11. Resentment, rebellion, and revenge (23 ")
12. Self-aggrandizement (166 ")
13. Self-gratification/ fame or position (42")
14. Self-exaltation (17 ")
15. Self-indulgence (58 ")
16. Self-pity (2 ")
17. Selfishness (94 ")
18. Sex and carnal desires (28 ")
19. Spite (2 ")
20. Stubbornness (5 ")
21. Suicide (4 ")
22. Vengeance (12 ")
23. Will and Willfulness (13 ")
24. Zealousness (6 ")

As you analyze this list, a few topics may rise to your attention, as they certainly did to mine! I wondered what was meant by "materiality," and discovered the following: "It may be said that the entity gained materially, though did not wholly advance spiritually or mentally.... Learn the lesson well, that an entity may indeed be rich in this world's goods and poor in his hope with his Maker." (Reading #3084-1)

"Misapplication" sounded intriguing, and Cayce's source gave a clear view of its definition: "Lost in taking sides and becoming so one-sided as to cause both wrath and madness to destroy the mental abilities of application of truths known." (Reading #97-2)

A sizeable stumbling block for many people is what Cayce termed "self-aggrandizement": that is, demanding for self without due consideration for others. It is a concept difficult to explain, and for many to comprehend. Cayce was asked to define the concept in simple words: Thus ever is will the factor in the application of what the entity has done or may do regarding the development of self in relationship to Creative Forces or energies. Simply, all depends upon how sincere self is as to its spiritual ideal – as to whether it is to indulge in the exaltation or gratification of self – self's own ego – or whether the soul or entity holds God as its ideal. If these influences are for self-indulgence, self-aggrandizement, self-exaltation without consideration to others, they become stumbling stones.

Note the linking of one's will and ideals to this question. Cayce encourages one to use "constructive and creative thinking," and to "think of others," and this will bring peace, beauty, and divine love.

As you may have noticed, part of the above list (How Souls Lost) represents behaviors and faults. Mistakes and faults are *within* the person; the fault often lies in *how* certain attributes of character or certain actions taken were used or misused.

Consider suicide, for example. This is a very delicate question and one of interest to many people, especially now that Dr. Kevorkian has made the national news by assisting individuals with terminal illnesses to die. The following quote implies that it is the *reason* for the action, not the action itself, that is crucial. "The entity lost through this experience, to the detriment of self, to the low dreg that of taking life in a way to satisfy self; not in defense of principle or of self, country, or position;..." (Reading #369-3)

With this solemn admonition, we shall leave the list of "losses" and proceed to the subject of how souls *gained.*

D. How Souls Gained

In 77% of all Life Readings, the source clearly stated how souls had gained in their previous lives. There is such a wealth of valuable information in this study that we can only hope to gather insights. Perhaps someday a more comprehensive study will be made by others.

A small sampling of how people were told that they had gained in previous lives follows: in the creative arts, in beauty, music, and entertainment, in not finding fault, in being a truthful keeper of records, in defending others, in love of story and adventure, in forgiving and being forgiven, in speaking and acting, by teaching, nursing, and in home, marriage, parenthood, an involvement with nature, and etc.

The Ideal is an important part of structuring a *future life*: "This will only be answered in self according to what it seeks as its ideal in such in its next appearance in the earth." (Reading #3611-1)

As important as the goal and concept of the ideal is in Cayce's work, it is also strongly stated that people cannot impose or force *their* ideals upon others. Example: "In the name then Harry Wortham, the entity gained, the entity lost, the entity gained in the setting of the ideal and lost in the trying to impose the same upon others. Be all ye should to everyone but impose not upon any. Rather be imposed upon than to impose." (Reading #5253-1)

Finally, the greatest areas of gain and growth take place in *patience* and *service to others*. The good we do for others is remembered always, for: "... the soul never forgets. For it is from the beginning and will be to and through eternity." (Reading #5346-1)

My research is based on 1,436 readings wherein the Cayce source stated how "the entity gained," approximately 350 readings of how "the entity lost," and 322 readings where "the entity gained and lost." Cayce practiced what he taught regarding the concentration on one's virtues and how one had gained, rather than getting stuck in how one lost or could have done better. Not only do Cayce's readings illuminate a person's past; he is careful to remind individuals of the future lifetime they are now building and preparing! Even though we may not see the fruits of our service and guidance to others in this lifetime, the seed is planted and will manifest in another lifetime.

For Mr. and Mrs. Cayce I hold the greatest respect and appreciation, because of their own lifetimes of patience and service to humanity. Based upon the research and study of my thirty years of experience at the Association for Research and Enlightenment I will state emphatically that, to me, Edgar and Gertrude Cayce were the most important pioneers of our century. Their fame was achieved not in the political or financial arenas, not as big-name media stars or the well-connected glitteratti, but as kind and patient healers in a world desperately seeking aid and succor.

This quote contains wise counsel for all: "For He the Lord of light, the way, the truth, the bright and morning star, the lily of the valley, the rose of sharon awaits – as has given His angels charge concerning thee – that thou walkest in the light. Be patient; for in patience, in waiting on the Lord, in being kind and gentle, do ye become aware of His presence in the earth. Not unto vaingloforying, but be ye joyous in the service that would make of thee in thy temptations – in thy trials – as one that would be a bright and morning star, a hope to thy fellow man, a prop to those that falter and stumble, a refuge to those that are troubled in body and mind!" (Reading #640-1)

Chapter IX
Love, Sexuality, and Spirituality

A. Gender Identity

There are many levels, degrees, and interconnections between love, sexuality, and spirituality. This chapter is more about soul lessons and forgiveness than it is about specific behavior patterns. While patterns will play a major role in the discussion of those topics, for now let us explore one of the most promising and dynamic aspects of life – LOVE.

Love means to console rather than to criticize, to hold rather than to withhold. Love is to look deeply into the eyes of the beloved – and with time to see there the reflections of past love and the vision of a continued future love. Love is to speak honestly together – even while the words are still forming – spontaneously, exuberantly. Love focuses on what builds, and builds. *Love* builds; trust builds; passion builds.

In walking the pathway that we call a lifetime, one encounters different views, different tests, different wonders. The path winds gently through the seasons. We meet other travelers, sometimes stopping to share a meal, a story, a smile. In their magical moments, lovers experience the enchantment of being together in the most intimate ways: the joy of living, the pleasure of coupling. The heart's memory bridges the gap between dimensions known and unknown.

During private sessions with my clients, questions concerning relationships arise more frequently than any other topic. This is because love, sexuality, and spirituality are in the forefront of our needs and experiences as humans. Sadly, all of those questions about relationships do not reflect positive or effortless experiences with others. Take a look at the current divorce rate and you will understand. Even so, divorce is not the real issue; it is only a symptom. Often, divorce is viewed as a failure, yet it can be a success, a true "graduation" – if the individuals involved are willing and able to heal and to forgive.

Later on in this chapter, I will share a case study of the difficult aspects of one individual soul's lessons and the work with forgiveness. His case is an example of a destructive pattern wherein he dragged others down with himself. But first, let us consider one of the most pressing questions of our time: gender identity.

In my research, I have noted that some people are concerned about having lived as a member of the opposite sex. It surprises them that virtually everyone has had lives in both genders. Regression work gives balance and meaning to this part of their larger selves.

Children often play at acting out different roles in their innocent games. When parents observe this, they may experience wonderful hints of past life memories emerging. Past-life patterns – strengths, talents, and problems – reveal themselves early in the present life. Young girls frequently will act out the masculine part of themselves, and young boys, the feminine. This is natural, healthy, and beneficial. With puberty and hormonal action, the sexual urges find direction.

In a reading in July, 1935, Edgar Cayce's source advised the need for a positive pre-teen sex education for all young people. His material was so revolutionary in its time that many would not accept its message. The overall theme of the Cayce readings is "wholism," that is, healing the entire person. The reading stated clearly that problems with sex manifested in adulthood stemmed from "...the lack of education in the young BEFORE their teenage years!" (Reading #826-6)

The test of time has proven this theory to be correct. Sex education has now become a standard part of the school curriculum. The need persists, however, for *better* education with a focus on the spiritual aspect of the body – as a temple of God – rather than a mere emphasis upon bodily hygiene. The more we learn about our sexual nature – especially if we are able to learn in the positive context that sex is healthy, vital, and alive – the more whole and happy we become. With further knowledge of this subject there will come a better understanding and the potential for growth, as we apply this knowledge.

The fear of discovering another of our past lifetimes as having been lived in the body of the opposite gender may manifest as the fear of becoming homosexual. Recent genetic research negates that fear. Gender urges, research reveals, are established long before birth. The genetic codes are clearly established and verifiable within the physical body.

In fact, past-life sessions may be an enormous asset in becoming less fearful of childhood memories and inner experiences. Many women have memories and dreams of having been men, just as many men have memories of having been women. Those early stirrings, vague memories, and odd feelings may be very confusing if one wonders whether one might be normal. This is, indeed, a far more common experience than one realizes.

Regressions bring balance to one's self-image and often result in healing at the sexual level. Past-life regressions emphasize that an existence as a member of the opposite sex *then* has little to do with the gender that we are *now*. It is significant only in the *memory's* experience, and not in the experience of the physical body. Each life is a new beginning. We learn and find wholeness by living lives in *both* genders.

In all of my research, one of the most intriguing discoveries was that in the more than 14,000 readings that Edgar Cayce gave, only a very few people had been of the same gender throughout *all* of their past lives. One of those people was a housewife, aged forty-nine years, who requested of Mr. Cayce a physical reading and a life reading, in 1943. She asked about her former lives in the earth plane. The reading told of her present life abilities as a teacher and instructor of young people while pinpointing the problems that she was experiencing regarding her husband's interference with her work:

"... we find ... a very exceptional entity ... innately and manifestedly ... a leader, a teacher, and an instructor for the young.... it would be well not to allow the idiosyncrasies of ... the husband ... to prevent the entity from fulfilling those abilities that are a part of the manner in which the entity may fulfill those purposes for which it entered this sojourn."

The reading continues with an admonition that this woman keep in mind, "... the business that ye entered the earth to complete...," and advised her to teach physical education to girls from six to fourteen years old "... as to their posture, their accent, their hairdress, their manner of clothing, their manner of study, their manner of adding consistently to the play, to the rest, to the work, to the activities that bring and keep the well balanced life; taking time to be holy in its correct relationship to sleep, to work, to play, to recreation, to study, and to application...."

The reading continued: "... The sojourns of the entity in the earth have been quite varied. Almost in each experience the entity has been an instructress, but in a different manner of presentation. For here again we find an entity every whit woman, not having changed its sex in its experiences in the earth. No wonder the entity doesn't understand men, nor men understand the entity. They cannot think in the same channel...." (Reading 3379-2)

When the time came for questions, the woman asked if she had been associated with her husband in previous incarnations, and was told that in the previous incarnation she had shared her life with this man, and that when she got rid of him, she got along much better. The source affirmed that she could do the same today. The woman was told that when marriage interferes with fulfilling one's life purpose, a disassociation or ending of the relationship is best.

Obviously, this was a most unusual case of a person who was out of step with the masculine aspects of her being, simply because of having always reincarnated as a female.

An understanding of *both* genders is a key that unlocks so many hidden mysteries. It holds much promise for the full evolution of mankind, and yet there is still confusion. It has been said, in jest, that mankind will never win the battle of the sexes because there is too much fraternization with the enemy. But times change, and we learn from new discoveries. There are historical precedents to be found in many eras and in many places which demonstrate the balance of masculine/feminine traits in everyone.

In *The Soul of the Indian*, Charles Alexander Eastman (Ohiyesa) explicitly portrays life in the close confines of the Indian home. In order to live together comfortably, careful procedures were followed and respected. The fiercest of warriors in battle were usually the gentlest within the home environment.

"No one who is at all acquainted with the Indian in his home can deny that we are a polite people. As a rule, the warrior who inspired the greatest terror in the hearts of his enemies was a man of the most exemplary gentleness, and almost feminine refinement, among his family and friends. A soft, low voice was considered an excellent thing in man, as well as in woman."

This statement profoundly suggests that a man confident of his strength and manhood need not "prove" it with ostentatious arrogance. He may enjoy the grace and peace of the homeplace because he is comfortable with his own masculinity.

In my three decades of regression, women – in past lives – tell of how their men were brutal and crude. Men relate how the women, on the other hand, were manipulative and complaining. It is my hope that, as a result of this research, people will grow to understand that both the male and female lives within each of us. Instead of polarizing ourselves to extremes, it is far wiser to study the strengths and needs of each gender. Women need emotional support to respond sexually. Men need sexual support to respond emotionally.

B. Sacred Sexuality — Passionate Spirituality

My work, and that of other researchers, has produced some positive – and surprising – insights. Some civilizations and cultures possessed a much better understanding and balance of sexual expression. (Research in this area alone is adequate to justify its own book, some day!) For now, let me share the fact that people from Polynesia and the South Sea cultures, the civilizations of ancient India, and many Oriental cultures – by and large – report healthier and more respectful expressions of sex.

In our mad rush toward technology, we have denigrated our emotions. Men tell me that they want to learn to become kinder, more gentle lovers, but there are few courses or classes which teach the spiritual aspects of sexual balance. Women tell me that they are tired of the crude male barbarians whom they have suffered for centuries. Some would rather be celibate than to endure such "lovemaking." Everyone needs and desires positive change in sexual interaction. The many torn relationships and bitter divorces that we see today affirm the need for change in our basic views regarding the importance and equality of both sexes and their interactions in love, sex, and spirituality.

Some clients are using hypno-regression to facilitate their return to those past times when their sexual expressions were more in harmony with loving actions. They wish to imprint those memories and to bring them back to the present time in order to reeducate themselves in the grace of more soulful and beautiful sexual interchange. Others work by building their spiritual lives with prayer, meditation, and self-hypnosis tapes. (Refer to end pages). By first building a spiritual life, one automatically builds a better life on all other levels, including that of sex.

There is a healthy link connecting spiritual development and sexual understanding. Some choose to refine their sexuality by applying a part of its creative energy to other interests such as art, music, dance, and/or poetry which, in turn, opens them to their fullest potential as sexual beings. The creative arts may assist in channeling sexual energy into spiritual expression. The more we refine our sexuality, the stronger is the development of our spirituality. The two are linked, for *all* aspects of life are an expression of the Creator.

C. A Life Out of Control

In past-life exploration, every sort of human experience comes to light – from the delicate and beautiful, to the very opposite. The following case-study demonstrates the downward pattern inherent in sexual lust and manipulation, the price paid for corrupting others, and the subsequent diseases that brought death and despair.

The man who came for this session was attractive and in excellent physical shape. He was a well-known and respected professional, dedicated to his family. Unfortunately, a divorce was looming on the horizon. As a result, this person discovered a critical need for insights regarding his spiritual or past-life history.

During the session he found himself in a past life in Europe, wearing well-made leather shoes that came up over his ankles, shoes with pointed toes. They were quite the style at the time. He was wearing dark-colored clothes under a cape. He had on a hat and gloves, as well as a belt of tooled leather and silver. He carried a sword and said that he sported a "sculptured beard." His story follows:

> "I'm in a city at night, breathing the air and feeling the power of the night – feeling like I'd like to be free, freer than I am," he said. In the next scene he states, "I'm sitting at a table in a grand ballroom before a huge fireplace. The table is laid out with fine silver cutlery and fine china....I'm having a meal with a beautiful woman and trying to seduce her.... I'm attracted to this woman because she has money.... She's attracted to me, so I'm 'playing' with her.

Throughout the dinner he attempted to manipulate her, drinking wine and using his psychic abilities to get into her head and to thus take advantage of her

weaknesses. He seemed to have an innate knowledge
of women, but misused that ability for his own dark
ends.

> "I've got several women who support
> me, take care of me, give me money and
> things – whatever I want.... I can easily
> manipulate these women, partly because
> I really please them sexually and they
> like that because their husbands are so
> brutal and insensitive to their femininity.
> But I know about that. I understand
> their femininity and I use that knowledge
> to get what I want. I don't really do any-
> thing, because I've developed this power
> to manipulate them.... I guess I'm sort of
> like a gigolo.... Some know about the
> others, but they don't mind because I've
> got such a psychic power over them.
> It's like an insatiable desire to totally
> possess their sexual essences and own
> that part of them, and that desire be-
> comes stronger and stronger.... It's a vi-
> bration right in my solar plexus area and
> it gets more intense as I play this
> game...."

Later in his life, he had developed his "game" even
further and spoke of having many women. They met
on a regular basis and he created rituals, very elabo-
rate rituals heavily charged with sex.

After years of such behavior, he found that he did
not like himself very much and this feeling began to

get to him. The peculiar power that he possessed now seemed to be out of his control, and was now controlling him. A part of him could not believe the actuality of what he was doing, but still he was driven by his insatiable lust for power, and for absolute dominion over women. As he neared fifty, there was no kindness remaining in him anymore, only meanness and the overwhelming need for total control. He wondered where it all would end and how far he would go. He even began to question what he was getting out of it, but seemed unable to stop.

Much later, he became so disease-ridden that he lived on pain killers but, despite the constant pain in his reproductive organs from the venereal scourge that gnawed at him, he was caught up in the web of his deceit – the pattern of his life – and could not escape.

As he became older and even more ill, he found himself alone in a room, his "guts all screwed up," and his digestion poor. He couldn't metabolize anything nor eliminate properly, and he had pneumonia. "I'm being poisoned....," he said; "... the body is poisoning itself."

There was a woman who, through all of this, loved him. He sent for her and she came because he was dying. She confronted him honestly with what he was and what he had done, and he accepted the truth; he craved that reflection of her wisdom and judgment. She spared him nothing:

> "You have exploited the sacred desire
> that God has given to humanity – the
> desire to experience oneness, unity, and
> completion between man and woman

...that sacred attraction that God has
given to man and woman to want to be
together in a warm, loving way.... You've
taken that and totally defiled it. Why did
you do that? Why? Look at the pain
you've created. Look at the pain you've
suffered yourself. Look at the marriages
you've ruined! What amazes me is that
some man didn't cut your head off – that
they didn't come to castrate you!"

This man's life in Europe had begun around the
year 1700 and he died sometime during the 1750's.
After his death, he passed into a space that was totally
dark, and with absolutely nothing there that he could
relate to – a void of darkness with no boundaries.
Nothingness. He experienced total despair.

With time, he reached an awareness of his terrible
deeds and reconciled himself to the incredible pain
and confusion that he had caused within that entire
circle of people. He accepted the fact that he alone had
created it.

"I brought forth that vortex of energy
and developed those powers, and I see
that that particular power is much too
dangerous to fool with.... I can't deal
with that one – sexual energy – because
it turned on me and controlled me.... It
turned me into an animal, an insatiable
animal."

I asked, "How do you balance that life with the

present? How do you heal that memory?" This person processed memory from an auditory mode, and so I suggested that he listen to the voice within and simply relate the answer as it came, without evaluation or forethought.

"How do I heal this memory in my present life? The way to heal that memory is to go within my heart and feel, tune into the love that I feel, the real love that I feel for my wife and the love and respect and reverence that I feel for all women, the incredible goddess within all women – tune in to that and feel that in my heart, feel that reverence and respect in my heart and feel gratitude for that awareness.

To heal this memory in my present life, my inner self.... What is its counsel? Integrate that feeling, that memory. Be more patient and allow myself to be, to remember, to feel the joy and the vibration in my heart of being loved, really being loved by a woman and being nurtured and trusted. To feel the joy of being trusted because in the past nobody trusted me; they feared me. And I've always felt I created situations whereby I wasn't trusted because there was no emotional security for a woman in a relationship with me. But just to relax...really...just step back and let myself, allow myself to feel the joy, the

> peace and the joy of being in a relation-
> ship where I am trusted."

I guided this man through a quite lengthy exercise
in forgiveness, and at last I asked about the woman
who came to him at the end of his life. He said,

> "Her name was Delores and she saw
> it all. She was an angel sent to me. She
> was ruthless in her reflection, but she
> held no condemnation."

Of the many thousands of actual case studies that
I might have included in this chapter, I chose this one
for its example of power – of its misuse and abuse.
This man paid a dear price for corrupting others, but
learned well his soul lessons and responded well to
the forgiveness exercises.

In his current life, this man is prominent in the
music industry and was able to come to my office for
only one visit. Had we been able to continue our work,
I am certain that a strong pattern linked to other lives
would have revealed itself quickly. I suspect that he
might have had a life – or lives – wherein he perfected
the sexual and spiritual gifts for the good; but,
throughout the European episode, he totally abused
that earlier knowledge and training.

Time is likened to a spiral, and we may either rise
on that spiral or fall. In this case study, we witnessed
a man spiraling downward like water being pulled
down a drain. He was not a victim, for he knew each
step of the way exactly what he was doing. He realized
that he had generated a power beyond his spiritual

evolution and had come to be controlled by it, becoming an "insatiable animal," spiraling down in a whirlpool of tragedy.

Fortunately, the wisdom and counsel from his higher mind gave him an insightful, practical, and therapeutic self-healing program. He learned a lot about Soul Lessons! Approximately one year later, I heard that the divorce did materialize, and I hope that it presented him with positive opportunities for betterment.

What is most important now is not to become angry with this man who so misused the sexual energy. Uncontrolled lust and terrible hurt are now common in our world. There is so much that we can learn from the deep memories within every person's mind. That is why I am such an avid researcher. THIS is the greatest area of learning and healing of our age!

Such work is linked to other major questions. As delicate a topic as it may be, the question of origins is vital to our study of soul lessons and patterns. It has been said wisely that rape is less a crime of sex than it is of dominance and power. Out-of-control dominance and rage often expresses in rape – the total opposite of that for which the sexual drive is intended.

Even sadder than the hurt and the craziness of rape is the implication that some of its victims later act out their hurt and become, themselves, a perpetrator. The prey may become the hunter and then the hunter (in other lifetimes) becomes, again, the hunted. Though completely polarized and at opposite extremes, the issue is still the same.

This is not to suggest that all rape victims become

rapists. Of course, they do not. Nor do all people who suffer rape bear the stigma of once having been a rapist. How absurd! There is a strong link, however, between what we experience and what we once "planted" or set in motion. The way to break any destructive pattern is to study and to heal the original cause – to go deeply into the causal time (through eons in the past) and to heal and to forgive the original people and circumstances involved.

Incest is yet another emotionally charged topic and one of the most terrible sins of our time. Incest is linked to the rape question, but it is turned inward upon the family and imprisoned there, hidden behind a facade of outwardly proper behavior. Is not its very secrecy an insult to the victim? Is the cover-up not an even worse crime, an abuse added to the hurt of the act itself? Again, the solution to such a crisis is to explore the past-life connections, the deeper roots of the pattern, and thus to help in healing *both* the victim and the victimizer.

Related to all of those questions – some of the most urgent of our time – is the underlying phenomenon of violence itself. Our nation has condoned family violence secretly by not publicizing its consequences. This aspect of the situation, at least, is finally changing.

Even so, in contrast to all of those positive changes that are being made, a certain amount of this much-needed publicity still might be construed as negative press. Some individuals have been hurt by publicity in a very different way – by being accused when they are *not* guilty. In my own field, perhaps unscrupulous therapists could have implanted or encouraged false memories. Even criminal prosecutors have alleged crimes against those who may very well never have committed them. Whether done for financial betterment, career advancement, or other sort of gain, those acts have cast a dark shadow upon the good work of those professionals who are ethical and conscientious in their intentions.

D. Love is the Answer

How do we move beyond the time-worn rut of patterns and into the fields of forgiveness and grace?

If once we enslaved others, now we work to free them.

If once we were cruel, now we sow the seeds of compassion.

If once we killed with the brutal strength of our hands, now we heal with the gentleness of those same hands.

If once we spoke in ignorance, now we choose our words more carefully.

If once we were scoffers and cynics, now we begin to trust our hearts.

If once we craved power for self-glory, now we strive to serve selflessly.

If once we demanded stature, now we humbly bend and graciously bow.

NOURISH YOUR SOUL

Artist: Jeffrey Winchester

Our present levels of love, sexuality, and spirituality are reflections or echoes of our earlier acts. There are deeper causes of, and greater meanings to, the events in our lives than we realize. We rise or fall on the spiral of time by our choices and our actions. Most people only consciously begin the process of healing once they have discovered their patterns. *Then* they are enabled to work out soul lessons and to practice active forgiveness.

Chapter X

Monks, Warriors, and other Extremes

A. Noble Causes — Terrible Consequences

In dealing with present-life and past-life patterns, I discovered my own weakness for going to extremes. For instance, in a series of lifetimes, I myself vacillated between the monk and the warrior. Such apparent opposites actually share a strong connection – a definite pattern.

As a monk, I enjoyed spiritual solitude; the quiet in my life was peaceful, simple, and reverent. Boredom brought out the warrior in me. This extreme swing from monk to warrior brought my involvement in wars or conquests which were sanctioned by the church and government.

For me, becoming a warrior in "religious war-games" was a total disaster! I thought it would be great, but it proved to be a terrible experience. I was told that we would be doing good; but we inflicted unspeakable horror. Conquests attracted the lowest strata of humanity with only a few idealistic people sprinkled in to give it the appearance of a noble cause.

The enemy was Bad, surely, but our own army was Worse! It was a terrible time for conqueror and conquered alike. I became disillusioned with the whole mess and vowed to return to the monastery.

But again, although the contemplative life was good for me, it lacked adventure and excitement. The warrior life was exciting, yet unfulfilling. Lifetime after lifetime my pattern formed. Invariably the pendulum swings between monk and soldier, then nun and victim of the army's lust, and again, between holy priest and gold-fevered conquistador.

More intriguing than my past-life pattern was my present attraction for others who shared my similar experiences. For example, most people are attracted somehow to those similar to themselves — or to their opposites. There are subtle unconscious signals or recognitions of persons with similar patterns. Simply stated, power-oriented people attract power personalities. Alcoholics easily attract other alcoholics. Victims easily attract other victims. It is apparent that similarities in past-lives attract people who shared those types of lives.

This phenomenon became apparent to me years ago in New England, when I had a big party at my home. As a Libra sun sign, I love any kind of get-together. I invited friends and asked them to invite THEIR friends – people I did not know yet. Many folks came; few wanted to leave. It was not planned to be a full weekend party, but we were all having such a good time that many guests stayed all night. Life-long friendships formed during that weekend.

While our party was indeed "fun," a larger event was taking shape. Quite unexpectedly, many of the people present had experienced past-life connections. In conversation and sharing, many became aware of deep connections or links to American Indian lifetimes. It was a spontaneous reunion of American Indian souls!

This theme was so strong that one person asked incredulously, "Has everybody had lives as Indians?" Well, nearly everyone at that gathering had, but not everybody in the world! As comic-relief to commemorate this unplanned and unusual event, someone dubbed it "Henry's Tribe." We all laughed. In that laughter there was balance, healing, and a subconscious reunion.

The long-term significance of that weekend is still unraveling. Our lives were touched in a most unusual manner. It is difficult to explain such subtle openings. One family who attended had previously shown no interest in the Indian legacy, yet, later were to become very prominent in the Indian movement. That family now works to preserve the sacred sites of Indians, and others, near Cape Cod.

B. Pattern Formations

Working with individual clients, and a few friends, I have encountered people with similar Monk/Warrior lifetimes. They encompass different nations and time periods. Recently, at a workshop, I was speaking about the Monk/Warrior pattern, and later received this letter:

Dear Mr. Bolduc:

At the "Life Patterns-Life Lessons Workshop" you discussed your monk/warrior pattern. I realized that I had a similar pattern in
my past lives.

In this present lifetime I've found myself
drawn to and repulsed by military matters. I
was in Army R.O.T.C. in high school and did
very well in the program. However, after graduation the prospect of going to Vietnam to engage in "real war" was frightening. I was fortunate to get into the army reserves where they
assigned me to the job of Chaplain's Assistant.
At the time I was amazed and bewildered because I had lost all interest in organized religion. After yesterday's workshop, it makes
sense – a warrior and a religious practitioner at
the same time!

After returning from active duty I
bounced from job to job never satisfied with the
work. Now, I've been working for almost sixteen
years at the Department of Corrections. This
has been both satisfying and frustrating. I believe my frustration comes from the monk/war-
rior pattern.

My spiritual work in an A.R.E. (Cayce)
Study Group is a great relief to the other work
that is my profession. I had other past lives
with similar patterns. One was a Taoist martial
arts master. More recently, I had a life in the
Shenandoah Valley of Virginia which I left to go
fight in the Civil War."

C. Pattern Recognition: The First Step Toward Healing

This letter, and others like it, attest to the realization that many people are aware of their patterns. Some patterns are obvious and others are subtle. Now that the writer of the above letter has recognized his patterns, he can begin the process of healing. Then comes enlightenment. There is no magic formula that is effective for everyone. As with any other kind of healing, the approach is unique for every individual.

As always, forgiveness is also the key in this situation. In subsequent sessions this person might begin to find ways to forgive himself and those whom he hurt or killed during the warrior times. He can work visually, auditorially, or be given kinesthetic tasks.

Following another workshop, a man wrote to me concerning his lifetime during the reign of Genghis Kahn. He had a certain pivotal memory – deep in his ancient heart. He had made a major decision to leave the violence, greed, and power of war forever. He moved to a higher plane both literally and figuratively, for good. He did not waver back and forth as I had so often done.

He wrote this account:

> "During the regression exercise I had to sit in the Zen position. I regressed to my life when unconditional love was the path to follow. I was at a pool of water where I washed myself completely, and went off naked to find my teacher. Starting from the pool, I walked off into the

hills and came to a small compound which was a school. I was not let in; but had to sit outside at the gate until it was 'time.' I sat in the Zen position; hence, the importance of starting the meditation (regression) in that position. I have no idea how long I waited, my impression is that it was several days. Finally, a small, older man came out. He fed me some thin broth from a small, wooden bowl. He then helped me into the compound and nursed me back to health.

"During my stay with these people, I learned the important path of life – that of unconditional love. I also learned to care for plants; whether for food or for spiritual growth, it could have been both. Then I was told that I had learned enough and had to leave. This was the saddest episode of my life. It was safe there and I felt love.

"I walked out the door and realized I was holding a staff in my right hand. I have had such a staff in another life as a monk, and also have such a staff at the present time. In my travels during that lifetime I came across a village which Genghis Khan had invaded. I was recognized as one of his leaders, brought to court and tried. It was my fate to be executed.

"I was bothered that these people didn't seem to understand that I had

changed. They had no concept of unconditional love. At least none except the executioner. He chopped off my head.
When he did so it was like chopping
through a head of cabbage. The sound
and feel were there.

"Then a great light bathed me, and I
realized that all the negative karma that
I had accumulated as one of Khan's
leaders was released. In one loving act,
the executioner had released all of it.
This was the happiest part of that lifetime. The executioner was very enlightened, and acted out of love. This kept
him clean as well. He had killed me out
of love and not anger or hatred as did
the rest of the court.

"Someday I may explore more thor-
oughly the life as a wandering monk to
see if I taught others. This truly was an
enlightening and cleansing experience.
When it is time for me to learn more I
will return. I thank the Spirit for letting
me complete and review such an important life as this."

Although those memories are of ancient times, the
feelings and learnings this man experienced were up-
to-date. This workshop participant gained further
understanding and information from his session. Such
understandings are like pieces of a puzzle which fit
together through time, with patience and work.

D. Evaluation from Within

Now, it is time to move to a different example of patterns: the patterns of extremes. Our next case study is about "Bill." Very big and muscular, Bill was in his early twenties and the possessor of a winning personality. He also was very active in the military reserves. His past life revealed a strong pattern of violence and destruction, which later balanced itself by reaping the very acts that he had sown.

Regression sessions vary with each individual. Some start off "choppy" with only random impressions and then move into a more flowing mode. Others begin by merely "looking back" as the detached observer, and move quickly into the re-living or "immersion" mode. Some people feel all the intense emotions of the past life. Bill experienced ALL of the above!

In our first regression session Bill easily encountered happy times from current childhood. We quickly moved to events prior to his present birth. All at once his countenance changed, and he was in a very different time and place, obviously.

"What are you wearing on your feet," I ask.

"Something like wrapping, almost like boots, almost up to my knees. They're made of leather and cloth and some metal." He describes plates of leather on his thighs and a lot of armor and swords on his arms and shoulders. "We're on horseback," he commented.

He was part of a very large army, riding hard into battle. They expected to slaughter the enemy in an easy win. They were exhausted but continued to penetrate enemy lines. It was very tense.

Bill continues in rambling thoughts; "Even if you don't kill one, we try to slip past him to the next one without being killed. The outcome of the battle is not so important, but the time when you are able to strike at just the right moment. If you lose your horse, you lose your life. If the horse must be sacrificed, all the time spent training that precious beast is lost. The horse does not ask to go to war, but merely serves. My horse died in this battle."

In a re-living mode, he exclaims, "My horse falls to the ground! I get off with my sword ready, but one of the enemy gets his spear into my back, twists it and rides with me still impaled on it. It hurts! It hurts where it entered my body. It hurts my whole body! I'm drenched with sweat. I'm afraid. Why me? Why? If only I had been looking the other way I would have seen him approach. I drop my sword just to bear the pain, while I hope no one else strikes."

I now interject to ease his agony. Using suggestion and detaching techniques I help him to release the pain and he then continues:

"Their second front comes over the hill and is more than we expected. It's easy for them to penetrate our ranks now. My friend jumps off his horse to help me — usually a deadly mistake. The one who stabbed me is now dead and my friend picks me up, carries me as if he is in no danger and simply walks and walks. It's very strange, the enemy just moves out of our way, even though we do not draw our weapons. He sets me down finally and bandages my wound. He gives me water and we rest. I know that I'm safe with him.

"We watch the battle, knowing our army will eventually win. Why do we do this? There's really no right or wrong – only that the strong survive."

We move to his old age and he sees himself as a near-barbarian among two young men of the gentry who are drunk and fighting. He tries to break up the fight, but they are disrespectful to him and deeply wound his pride as an old soldier. He draws his sword when one of them challenges him, and out of sheer anger runs him through, delivering a fatal wound.

"I have killed one of the gentry's sons. I wonder if they will remember that I am the one who fought their battles and trained their young men. Will they recall that I have sacrificed my entire life for their wars? Or will they consider me a common criminal? The *new* army is honored. They are well trained, but inexperienced. They are considered the better army, but I know they are soft. I have refused to give up my old ways, the ways that have worked all of my life.

"I am to go before a panel of elders at whose tables I have sat and discussed plans of war. They are very powerful people. Some say they are magic. They are odd looking, very white and dressed in white. Some are extremely blond, almost albinos, with long limbs and long fingers. Each is thin and frail looking, but very wise.

"Among these judges is the father of the young man I killed – he is the whitest of them all. I know him, but I did not recognize the youth as his son.

"He believes what I say; he knows that his son tried to strike first. He is grieved. He is, of them all, the most fair in judgment. The others follow his decision, for he is not only an elder, but the father of the deceased.

"They are all much older than I, and very mysterious, but they do not look down upon me as does the generation that follows them. It does not matter to them that I refuse to become part of this "new" army or that I choose to remain a savage as I learned in the large army of my youth. They know I have not much time left because of my advancing years. They know, too, that their civilization will spread and prosper without the need for large armies."

I am not sure why I was interested in asking about the time and place of the life. Bill, in his current life, probably was unaware of an ancient continent of Atlantis; however, during the session he explained that this life was in a colony of Atlantis. He was in a new city away from the main continent, located south of the Mediterranean. He watched the colonists' construction as they used great machines, and was amazed at what they could do, saying; "I did not understand the science behind all this, nor was I interested. I had already become a highly respected warrior."

It was evident that he cared little for the trappings of civilization, and wanted to talk of war and battles. I asked him to continue.

"My friend, Negan, survives many battles with me. He is of equal rank and saved my life more than I saved his. We would not be in the city long, for they need us farther east. We have already come in here and fought the hardest battles while the gentlemen of the new army ride in to claim victory. They send us ahead in small groups, assuring themselves that we will be killed off, relieving themselves of having to deal with us 'barbarians.'" He was embittered!

I questioned what the most important event of

that life was. "The travel – when Negan and I go east on our horses, traveling hard into another battle. We can live like barbarians and be happy, knowing we fight much harder than the others. There is still much anger and senseless killing. I never married in this life. There's no need – if I want something, I take it. I wish I had had children though. I like children. But, I am old now, and war is the only thing left to do. There's one last battle. Negan receives a fatal wound and is left to die. The resistance is close and I no longer care. I ride hard into battle. I simply put my arms out to my sides and let myself be run through by another spear. I can accept death; I no longer care about the battle. Without my friend it isn't fun any more. We were going to be together in death. I don't care about the new civilization and the new mannerisms. Negan's death, or my dying, is no longer important. We are merely giving in to the flow of things, that's all."

I asked him to look into the eyes of his companions to send them love and blessings, to release them and to allow them to fade. When I guided him through this process with the one who had killed him, he recognized that soul from the present life.

About this he said, "We were literally at each other's throats for years, one always waiting for the other to make a mistake fatal enough that he might kill the other, even in this current lifetime. We were always opposed. I was willing to kill him for so long. Now we must make amends."

Once again I interject and guide him through forgiveness exercises. Exercises vary from person to person. Sometimes we experience various modes of forgiveness and release. At other times I leave it to the individual to suggest the best course of direction, i.e. "What can *you* do to balance and to heal this situation?"

I then asked Bill to step above that life into the perspective of universal time to tell what the lessons were – what he had gained and had understood.

"All the so-called "progress" is not always better. All these cities being built meant nothing, for people grew more and more arrogant and further away from each other. And, the further apart they grew, the weaker they became. I was with my friend – we were all an army of friends. *The friendship is the important thing, knowing that someone is always with you. The unity, the bonds of human relationships – that was the important thing.* You can't put a price on that. That was the lesson."

We were just ready to finish this session, returning him to the present, when he came upon another scene. He was with a young girl who loved him and was sad when he had to leave for battle. He had deceived her into thinking that he would take her with him for, when he was called, he left abruptly.

"I did not tell her I would be leaving soon. I was sad that I had taken advantage of her, forgetting that the bond was the most valuable thing. That was a mistake from that lifetime."

Although Bill, in his current life, was in his early twenties, the man from his past life had great wisdom, even though his role or persona in that time was barbaric. Again, we worked with forgiveness and the release of the young woman whom he had deceived.

For perspective, this session was conducted about fifteen years ago. It was my custom at that time to allow witnesses or friends to sit-in during the sessions, by way of informally teaching others and demonstrating the efficacy of regression work.

An observer at this session was moved to tears by the intensity of the loneliness expressed on losing his best friend. At the depth of Bill's remorse over failing to recognize the bonding between himself and the young girl, there was an almost palpable empathy exhibited by those in attendance. When we worked together to apologize and to send love, a general lifting was felt by everyone present.

Bill also shared with us the feeling that earlier, when I had guided him to let go the intense physical pain of his wound, he vividly had felt the sensation of electricity throughout his arm and the rest of his body. He broke out into a sweat. Somehow, when the weapon entered, the pain was so intense throughout his entire body that it was as though he were weak and vulnerable to anyone else who chose to attack him.

"I've noticed that most of my lifetimes have been just war after war," he commented. "There was never any question in my mind that I was going to be part of the military in my present life. It was just a matter of waiting for the right time. I'm really glad now that I stayed with the Reserves."

At a later session, Bill and I worked together again, this time video taping the session. In this regression he went back to a female life. Even here, the old pattern was to haunt him, or more accurately *her*.

She was barefoot in a foggy, rainy, cold place, wearing a little brown animal skin. She had tiny white legs and her arms were exposed. The animal skin which covered her was inside-out so that the softness was on the inside, making it warmer. She was standing on a moss-covered rock, watching the ocean splash around her. Other children and older people were rooting around, beneath and between rocks for food.

When I moved Bill to a later time of that life, he said, "We're in a small, crowded tent in the grasslands; no longer near the ocean. We're all listening to our leader. We're scared because invaders come and soon we will have to leave to find a safer place. Our leader fears all of us will die!

I asked about the invaders and learned that they came from the East. They were dark-skinned with black hair and black eyes. They had traveled a long way looking for a home. The invasion and possible war was eventually to disrupt her life completely.

"There are many of them..they do many cruel things if they catch you, but we always manage to escape because we are so few and we can move faster. We go northeast to plan how we may fight back some day."

They moved to a mountainous, barren land where they survived by hunting. They made their homes in caves. They boast that their leader has more fur, more metal, more gold, and he's proud again. He's proud, for they feel more secure with iron, swords, and steel.

The cave homes are adequate. "There's water inside the caves. Water that's hot, even though it's cold outside. You can bathe in it; the pools are deep."

Then, when she was a little older, "The king is angry with me that I won't do what he says. My parents are dead and he wants me to call him 'Father' and I won't. I won't be his daughter..His children are dead..I'm glad he is my leader, but I can't be his daughter. I am very, very beautiful with long, blonde hair..he wants people to think I am his daughter, but I can't do that to my parents, even though they're dead.

"He gets angry and tells me if I won't be his daughter, then I must leave..I'm thrown out during the worst of the winter. Banished! I walk outside the cave down the steep ledges and I see my friends. They bring me to another cave where I won't be found..many fear the leader because he's lost his sanity. Then, a young man kills him with a knife and pronounces himself king. He is younger than I, but I know that he wants me. I would gladly be his wife, even though he's only fourteen. He is courageous and wants to lead us back through the mountains to go south again.

"We reach the valley and see fields of tall grass. We decide to stay because we don't know where the enemy is. We build houses of stone, granite actually, and make a village for the twenty of us who have come.

"Three years later, some go south, and when they return they report that the enemy has gone. They have traded some iron for cows, bringing them back to us.

The young families began another generation in the village, and she continues by describing their life: "There are little children running around..our house is barely tall enough to stand in, with a table and chairs and rough plates and mugs. Men come in and talk to my husband. The children run all over with their energy until I'm too tired to chase them anymore. We don't try to restrict them because they're small. We

don't want them to know what it's like to have to run
and be afraid. So, we let them run freely. The village
is cold and the winters hard. Many leave to return
south to the sea, among them our cousins. There are
only four or five families left who stay. Our cousins
visit occasionally and tell wonderful stories about the
sea. My children listen and grow dissatisfied, wanting
to go. Everyone wonders why we stay here. We don't
know either, it's just our place. It's better than the
caves. We are too tired to move everything again, so we
just stay. Our children go with my cousins to the
South."

I move Bill up to the time of death in that life and
ask for a description. "After the children go, I'm sad.
Only three families are left. Life is not easy here, but
it's pleasant. There's really not much reason to go on.
Nobody lives long anyway. Maybe I'm thirty-five. The
children were twelve or thirteen, old enough to leave,
so I let them go. That was many years ago, and I'm
just lying here wondering what they're doing. Why did
we ever stay, and thinking what was the purpose of all
this pain and running and hardship. I just sort of die
of loneliness, of a broken heart. I lie there and think
and pretty soon I'm just looking at myself, contemplat-
ing. I see my husband come in and he knows that I
am dead.

"I just go away from that little stone house, but I
don't know where to go next. I remember the caves
and the hot water when I was young and beautiful. I
see myself playing on the rocks, with my skinny little
white arms and legs and my tiny feet, jumping and
smiling, a happy little girl playing on the moss, smelling the ocean. But, there's someone standing there

looking at me. I can't really see him, he's like a shadow standing there, he looks almost like our king. He wants me to follow him.

"I walk up to him and he smiles, and I'm a little girl again with the skinny legs and arms, the tiny teeth and very blonde hair. 'Valhalla,' he says, and then everything is gone."

I then asked Bill to rise to a point where he could see this lifetime in its full perspective, and to tell me how his soul grew from this, and asked him what he had gained.

"Free will and destiny," he said.."always do what your will wants and don't control the will of others..not to become the daughter of a man you don't want as a father and not to make your children stay where they don't want to be...allowing the two wills to live together in peaceful coexistence."

About a year later Bill had another regression that took him to a time rather close to the present, again filled with violence. He was, again, a woman named Becky, about nineteen with long blonde hair. Becky found herself in the passenger seat of an old car on a very hot night. Something seemed to be wrong – steam coming from under the hood, the radiator too hot. The driver, a man she knew called Johnny, about twenty-three, seemed very frightened as this trouble started, forcing them to pull off to the side of the road in a very isolated area. She suddenly heard a very loud noise, like thunder, and before they had time to realize what it was, a motorcycle gang came up on either side of them. They dragged Johnny out of the car and as-saulted him with a crowbar. He could not defend him-self against them all. She locked the car doors to try to protect herself. They broke the windows and dragged Becky and Johnny into a field.

"They're crazy, like animals, all of them screaming. They pull us both into a field. Johnny's almost dead, there's blood all over his face where they have hit him, they're gonna kill him."

It was necessary to interrupt Becky to help her to release the image and pain and fear. I was about to guide her out of that session when she said, "There's more." So I let her continue.

"I can't see it, but I know it happened. There was indescribable pain, I know it happened, and I know that we were both killed and left there. No one knew; or maybe they did know, but wouldn't stop whoever did it. Maybe they were too scared..I'm just drifting away in the morning from that field, floating away from it..I can see the car now, but I'm just lifting, going away from those two bodies, dead."

I guided Bill out of hypnosis, and we settled into discussion. Bill confided that he had had dreams about this experience and would awaken with fragments of images. He said he dismissed them as bits of different movies that he might have put together.

"This time," he said, "it was very clear that we were just dragged into that field...I never knew previously if I was the girl or the guy..but it's so much clearer now..I believe it was around 1959."

This session was observed by a large group of people who witnessed the re-experience of a violent rape by a gang of wild, drunken men AND women. I personally had the secret suspicion that some members of the gang were souls of those people Bill had violated in a similar manner in previous lives. If so, this is a clear example of going to both extremes to learn balance and counter-balance.

For those same souls, I believe, the distance in linear time between their roles as victim and victimizer may have spanned hundreds of years.

Theories abound as to why some souls return to be born so soon after their deaths, or why others wait many years or even centuries to return. Perhaps further research will bring light to this and to numerous other questions about those fields of discovery.

Bill was born in the early 1960's. When we started our work he was already a big, physically fit young man, exceedingly strong and active in the military reserves. The military life had always fascinated him. He confided that he owned and carried within his vehicle a large number of firearms. "I knew, deep within, I would never be vulnerable again. As Becky, I was defenseless and outnumbered. We were at the wrong place at the wrong time. I guess it was an experience of being the victim instead of the victimizer – different from my usual pattern."

In the field of therapy it is wisely said that a therapist should never explain a parable if the client does not perceive it on his own. This means that the purpose of a story or metaphor is meant to hint at meaning and wisdom. Should the wisdom be perceived, fine. If not, then, apparently the time might not be right, or the client might not be ready for change. Those same general guidelines are appropriate for the recognition of past-life patterns. Such realizations must come first from the client. Then, and only then, should the therapist or the facilitator further discuss and help to evaluate one's patterns.

In Bill's case, he quickly grasped the larger picture of his lives. He first saw the pattern of re-running an involvement with war, then its opposite extreme of becoming the victim, somehow balancing his experiences.

We have insight into four of Bill's lives – three past ones and the current life. Some patterns are obvious and some are subtle.

Which can you detect? Even more interesting is his present-life career or profession. He left the military reserves and is now a Security Guard. How ironic that in the past he brazenly took other's possessions. In this life, he now protects the possessions of others.

Bill's work took him to a distant part of the country, and I have not seen him for over a decade. If someday we are to continue the work, I am sure that he will also relate one or more monastic life experiences. I have no tangible proof for that belief, but years of experience suggest its validity to me.

The connection between warrior and monk is stronger than I would have ever guessed when I started with research. For me, personally, it has been most helpful to recognize those extremes. I no longer bounce back and forth. I maintain balance and fulfill my spiritual work by giving workshops about the spiritual purposes of life, not as a priest or a monk, but in the hustle and bustle of everyday life. I have discovered better reasons to travel not to plunder and to kill, but journeying to bring messages of hope and to help guide others on their path to enlightenment.

For me, the answer is to travel between the extremes and to experience adventures while doing the spiritual work. Each must find his or her own path, whether outward and active, or inward and contemplative. Perhaps one must travel both roads concurrently!

It may require courage and strength to be a warrior. I feel, however, that it takes greater courage to be a spiritual adventurer, to teach peace instead of violence, wisdom instead of foolishness, and generosity instead of greed. Devoting your life to such pursuits and life-styles presents a larger, richer image on your soul-screen than many could imagine.

More than anything else, regression work has taught me that there is a fine line between courage and stupidity. Often, the two extremes are hard to identify, for we mask them with nice-sounding phrases: "Fight for Peace," "Department of Defense" or "The Peacemaker" for deadly missiles. Such examples only hint at our national mentality, that of being a very aggressive nation with a giant military budget!

We can ask such questions at the individual level also. What is true courage? Should we hurt people for their own good – to "teach them lessons?" As I perceive it, courage is the strength to face every situation with wisdom. Gentleness is not weakness; strength is not gained by being a bully.

Perhaps the most courageous thing any person could do is to explore his or her own mind! Everyone has a mind, but most people are afraid of examining it! It is said that people fear most what they least understand. One's own mind must surely qualify in that case!

The inner mind is, indeed, a great frontier. Earth's lands are mapped, the seas already sounded, even the solar system has been probed. Why is the mind a sacred mystery that frightens so many? Mind is the door to the past and the window to tomorrow. Thank God, there are courageous explorers and map-makers willing to pioneer!

Chapter XI
Healing the Past

A. Three Case Studies

The healing of any problem or situation begins with its detection and analysis. The following chapter contains the case studies of three individuals.

1. Case Study #1: Claire

Claire, the first study, came to me for spiritual reasons and not for therapy. She was not seeking the origins of any patterns. As you will see, however, strong patterns quickly became evident.

Although I did not ask her to transcribe the cassette tapes of her sessions, she felt that the process of copying or writing the words from each tape was a process that offered insights of great value.

Claire and I developed a friendship over the years, and when I asked her to make a chart of the first six lives we had explored she put them in the order remembered, not chronologically. She persevered and reduced an entire lifetime to a single paragraph, using her own words in each chart. The Case Study #1 which follows is my explanation of the sessions. Since completion of this chart we processed one other life where she was the victim of epileptic seizures. The local people thought she was possessed.

After completing the chart she was able to see clearly the various lives, their lessons and problems. Then, I asked her to list any patterns she perceived. She found nine. Perhaps you can detect more. The number of patterns is not nearly as important as the LESSON of each pattern. I felt, also, that it was important not to offer suggestions at this point, but to let her discover her own patters.

These are her patterns:

1. Service to others
2. Leadership ability
3. Pride
4. Spiritual focus
5. Psychic tendencies
6. No family – never married
7. Self reliant
8. Difficulty in being open or trusted
9. Three lives with no mother

Our work is on a continuing basis. On an average we have done one session per year. That number might seem low to some, high to others. There is no set number of regressions needed in order to be effective. I caution, however, to proceed slowly and wisely in order for each person to assimilate the lessons and patterns of each lifetime. I counsel many more seekers to "slow down" in their inner search than to speed up.

I smiled at an Edgar Cayce reading which I found wherein a person asked, "What qualities must I develop to grow more rapidly, spiritually?"

Cayce's one word answer explained it all, "Patience!" (Reading #2981-1, Q&A #6)

Life	Mountain Girl	Dumb Warrior (Male)	Orphanage (Woman)
Synopsis	Mother died in childbirth; physically and emotionally abused by father. Precognitive dreams caused her to be labeled evil. Left home when father died. Lived in town with aunt until she died. Girl decided she harmed those whom she was around and chose to live her life back in mountains. As a recluse, no friends except animals. Died as old woman — killed by a bear.	Leader of his village. Was a very strong and big man. He was captured by another group of warriors, and his people were killed. He was tortured — his fingers were cut off one by one, then his arm, and he was left in the center of the village to slowly bleed to death. He refused to cry out during torture. He was too proud to let anyone hear him cry or scream.	Mother died in childbirth. Father gave her to a man when she was about 3 years old. Man was a "man of One God" and ran an orphanage. Girl grew up and helped man run orphanage and took over when he died. He taught her about the One God when her father and people believed in many gods. She was sitting with him as he died and saw his astral body/soul leave his physical body at death.
Gain	• Affinity with nature and love of animals • Psychic • Self reliant	• Courageous • Concern for others (his villagers) • Inner strength	• Faith in God • Life of service to others
Problems	• Insecure • Afraid to be with others • Hated father	• Pride • Distrust of others • Stubborn	No problem areas surfaced for this life.
Current Life Reflections	• Reserved, difficulty meeting people • Love of mountains and animals • Psychic tendencies	• Pride • Leadership ability • Inner strength • High tolerance for pain • Tendency to hide feelings • Difficulty trusting	• Concern/care for others • Good with children • Strong faith

Eskimo (Male)	Mercenary (Male)	Priestess (Female)
Leader of village. Considered spiritual contact and authority. Villagers were starving. He had let his pride interfere with God-connection, but hid this from people. He left village telling people he had a vision of where to hunt for food. Untrue. He left with no intention to return because he had lost his power and was too proud to let anyone know. He sat down in the snow and cold and chose to die rather than admit failure.	Grew up as an orphan eating garbage in alleys. Very angry. Distrustful. Eventually led army. Did not care for anyone. Just concerned to be a good soldier. Was killed on the battlefield. Died angry because someone had made a mistake and let army be trapped with river at their back.	Was taken at age 3 to live in temple and train to be priestess. Life spent teaching, healing, and much time spent meditating and praying. Helped people who took refuge in temple during earthquake. She was caught under fallen building in her room. As she died her concern was for those she heard crying for help and sorrow that she could not help.
• Leader • Spiritual • Love, nurturance of others	• Self reliant	• Life of service • Healing • Faith/spiritual • Teacher
• Pride • Loss of faith • Self centered	• Callous distrust • Anger • Arrogant • Distrust of others	This life seemed to have no personal problem. This life was lived according to plan established before birth.
• Pride • Not open with others • Spiritual	• Difficulty trusting	• Faith • Care of others • Teaching ability

Claire is a retired college teacher with a long-term interest in psychology, hypnosis, and self-hypnosis. She had read my book, *Self-Hypnosis: Creating Your Own Destiny*, which discusses making self-hypnosis tapes, and had hoped to find someone nearby whose ideals were similar to her own. A mutual friend surprised her with the fact that I lived only a few hours away. She wrote to me promptly, and we set up an appointment. She arrived ready and enthusiastic for her first regression.

In hypnosis, I asked her to go to age eighteen and to relate a happy occasion. She was unable to recall a single one. She could remember only feeling anxious to get away from her mother. I continued guiding her back, and found that even at age four she was very sad. She felt "out of place" with her family. She was close to tears, and I sensed a period full of conflict.

We continued back through the years until we came to gestation in the womb. She became very agitated. She declared, "I'm really not meant to be in this family. This is not what I'm supposed to do."

Leaving this whole period, I gently suggested she go back into a past life. She brought forth an experience in which she was an extremely unhappy young girl with two older brothers. Her mother had died giving birth to her, leaving her to suffer her father's resentment. After her father's death, she left the hills and her hostile brothers to go to a nearby city to live with an aunt and uncle. The aunt did not want her, but the uncle took her in to live with them in exchange for work.

One night she dreamed of her aunt falling down the stairs and dying. Later, when it actually happened, she blamed herself, thinking that in some way she had caused it. She decided then that in order to avoid harming those around her she would return to the hills to live in seclusion. The animals became her only friends, and she vowed never to eat meat. In later life she was killed by a bear. She was ready to die, feeling her life had no purpose.

After death, she went in spirit to visit her brothers. She had not seen them since leaving the hills years earlier. Her presence frightened them; one almost had a heart attack.

During this session she experienced much self-healing, and was able to bless and to forgive her father. Her purpose in that time, she found, was to learn to let go.

In discussing her current life insights, some interesting points arose. She remembered being told that her birth was breech and very difficult. She was not breathing, and the doctor labored over her to start life. Her mother had revealed that for three months she was a colicky, screaming baby.

Claire realized that some patterns were becoming more clear: that meat is a very low priority in her diet; that she has always been independent, self-sufficient and solitary; that she has long recorded her dreams; and that her relationship with her domineering mother has been most difficult.

Her first session was so emotionally charged that I suggested she not rush back for other sessions. She diligently studied and transcribed her first tape. After five months, I was aware that she was a mature and well-adjusted person, and I felt that it was time to continue.

In our second session, after putting her through a hypnotic routine, I asked about her function and destiny for the current lifetime.

"...I am being told that it is time for me to start my journey, to bring light to others, and this is my purpose on earth at this time.....I chose the mountains of Kentucky, the fundamental background, the strictness of discipline in which to be reared, that others may know that there are no limitations fixed upon the soul...if the will is aligned with the will of God and you follow the path the soul has designated for the life, then you can truly meet the light at the end of the road. The way is being cleared for me. Reluctance of the consciousness to expose self to ridicule has been the drawback. ...Open the way; release all that is unnecessary in life; go forward. This is the message...the purpose...the way."

Regarding past lives pertinent to her present spiritual development and destiny, she said that her search had progressed. She had come to this point in time and had suffered the events in order to make known the feelings that can be overcome. At times, her search had been rigid, within the confines of the church, but she felt that she did not fit in with the established rules and chose to follow her own path to God. Many times she did nothing, but searched in vain, unwilling to release material items she possessed. "The more you release," she said from her hypnotized state, "the more you gain."

Her primary lesson for this lifetime is to understand the transient nature of material possessions, which she has been given in abundance. "They have no meaning. What has meaning is love and light...it is time to go back to the spirit, to let the spirit manifest, and know that once the will has been surrendered all will be there, not just love and light, but the material things of this life also. It is not God's will that anyone should suffer deprivation or do without. All that needs to be done is to recognize that the Father supplies all needs. Dependence must be put where dependence can do good, and that is on the soul."

Four months later, Claire returned for a regression session in which she processed two lifetimes. I could tell by our conversations that she was working diligently between sessions, quite determined in her growth.

The session began by uncovering what seemed to be an American Indian life, as she spoke of her pride in the moccasins she made. "I'm really very good at making moccasins...," and she proceeded to describe the rest of her clothing.

Suddenly, there was an abrupt change to an earlier or different life. I had assumed that in the "Indian" time she was female, but in this different life she was now a male. "I'm a man," she stated in a deeper tone with a more self-assured manner. She described her hairy legs, big shoulders, powerful arms, the helmet with horns she possessed, and added, "I'm strong, but not smart."

This session was virtually a monologue. There was no need for me to ask questions. She had fully entered the experience, which is rather typical by the third regression experience when an individual is comfortable and trusting of the process.

"I rule with might. I am a son of Thor. I'm proud of myself, and no one dares oppose me. I am a great warrior." The warrior describes the village, the huts, the women cooking. Then, suddenly, there is a stir as others intrude on horseback. Everyone is running to hide.

"I am a prisoner. We had no horses. They try to break my spirit. I pretend." Much pride and arrogance remain in the voice and attitude.

Mentally I note the contrast of this trait and manner with that of the woman, Claire, who is the epitome of southern gentility.

The warrior's people are treated worse than the cattle as they toil in the fields. "Better to be dead and free than alive and captive," he muses.

They plan an escape but are caught trying to execute it, after someone informed the captors. The chieftain's reward will be a special hell before he is allowed to die...he is to be made an example.

"They are dragging me through the streets," he says, pain twisting his face. "...a sword ran through my side..great pain, but I refuse to cry out." Then, "..my fingers..my fingers..they are chopping off my fingers one by one..." Then, "They have severed my arm..I lie in a warm pool of my own blood, numbed by pain..."

He is left overnight to die in the square. "Just to die..just to die and find peace..I was the example..no one else will run away.." He expels a long, deep breath, then seems to die, "...I am free. I can see me..it's my body, but it's not me..I'm above it..I die but I'm not dead..!"

In death the warrior cries, "My God, I need help..My God..Ah, I see a messenger..he comes on a horse..I will rest and sleep. I have no need for this warrior image any longer..I shall shed it..I'm home. This is my place..my peace. I would wish never to inhabit a physical form again, but that is not to be. We must strive and grow..and learn our lessons."

Now I ask Claire, "What happens next in your soul's journeys?" Still in hypnosis, her voice describes meeting next with three persons to determine what will be beneficial for the warrior in his search. They help him to review the lives left behind and the possible lives ahead, in order to choose carefully. Yes, there is choice: it's called "Free Will." "They encourage me to grow in knowledge and to use my time wisely..here and in the next life I must live."

They show Egypt. "No," Claire says, "I do not wish to."

I notice now that Claire is rubbing her fingers together and continues to do so for the rest of this session. I wonder to myself if this is at some level just to feel her fingers intact after having just experienced their loss in the life just reviewed.

Finally the soul chooses to become part of what it calls an ordinary family in Egypt because there is much love there. "I choose to be born again. There is one large room and a room upstairs as well." Everything seems happy and positive. Then suddenly Claire cries out, "Oh God! Oh, God!" Her mother died giving birth to her. She evaluates the situation herself without any questions from me. Despairing, she sighs,

"Another life without a mother's love and care. I am a female child, but the love is gone. There is no love in this family now, only emptiness. I take away the love..I destroy that which made my life possible."

I remember that her mother had also died in childbirth in the life reviewed in our first regression session.

She continues by telling that her Egyptian father gave her away to a man who came to their house. "He is a good man. He takes good care of me. I have food to eat and clean clothes to wear. Why did he want me? There are many here. He tells us stories of the One God..he must be wrong..my father worshiped many gods..how can there be just one?"

The question of the One God presents a major conflict for her in Egypt. Later, after much self-interrogation, she changes the subject. "I have duties to perform, but they are not bad. Why was I chosen by this man? When I ask him, he says he saw me in a dream. Is this possible?" Again, she processes a lengthy monologue about this fact.

She moves on to the old man's deathbed. "I set there and watch him die. He is not sad..he is at peace." She screams, "Oh, God, I see him leave! I *see* him leave! How is this possible? Have I truly lost my mind? I don't dare tell anyone! How is this possible?"

Finally, she nears her own end. "I have spent many years here caring for the young." I assumed the place to be an orphanage or temple school for training children. After she evaluates the life, we do an exercise of looking into the eyes of the people from each life and sending love, blessing, and forgiveness.

This was an insightful session because it showed

the two extremes of lives in one single session: the arrogant and proud warrior who died unyielding, and the girl born to a life of service to humanity and taught the love of the One God.

Claire recalled little, if any, of this session upon awakening. The interesting aspect of her series of lives is the soul perspective she has about each life. This is effective *self-healing*.

Claire's fourth session began with tears from the present life at fifteen years old. She felt she did not deserve to be happy in life. She had met a young man at a small party, and he liked her. She reasoned that if he liked her, there must be something wrong with him.

Entering once again into the regression state which she had come to experience, she finds herself in a very cold land wearing furs. She is a male with yellow skin and black hair. Although neither of us realized it at the time, this session began near the end of that life. As in other sessions, there was almost constant hand movement throughout.

This man is in a desolate place. He has a vision of a green forest, an "enchanted forest." He considers escaping to this forest, but is confused and reluctant about going. He faces a choice between lying down to allow peace to come, or returning to his village. He decides. "It is time. We always know when it is time."

From the dimension of death, he considers it was a good life with much to be thankful for, an experience that was easy enough. I guided him to the place of the Eternal Self, or the Superconsciousness. We had been here before at this highest level of awareness and had achieved much insight.

But this time it was different. The man had thought it was a good life, but the "Eternal Self" saw it differently. In fact, the comment was that this life had been a major defeat, a total tragedy. The entity had had the ability to communicate with God in the same way in which the "Shamans" do today. Messages came through him for the people and the village itself. He was allowing his soul to slip away from this gift of communion with God, however. Pride and arrogance were building as the leader gained more power and influence over the people. As his life progressed he had found it necessary to cover up the fact that this spiritual connection was no longer there.

"I talked to God. I was the mediator for my people. Each day I received messages and I guided my people by them, and I had peace and purpose. I lost that. I knew I had lost it; so when I left my village, I told them that I was being led to the great kill that would feed the entire village. I knew I would not go back to them. I could not return because I could no longer receive the word. It was time for someone else to take over. My brother, who had been trained to listen, could take over. They will miss me, yes, they will miss me."

The soul records said that he had lost touch with his life's purpose and, "...rather than humble self, he chose the coward's way out."

How ironic that although the man's subconscious pronounced this life a good life, his superconscious declared it as *tragic*. As Claire lay hypnotized, the higher self spoke through her strongly: "This one was chosen from birth with the knowledge that he would lead the people he chose with whom to incarnate. He would bring them to the knowledge of God and com-

munication with God. Through pride and arrogance
the God-connection weakened. The village that could
have been prosperous was left destitute. This leader
had a conscious *knowing* that if he released the physical he could return to the light. He chose to abandon
life instead. Thus, much karmic debt was encountered. It was a sad ending to a life so full of promise
and opportunity."

When questioned about the lessons learned or
debts incurred, the answer came back: "There must be
much study and inner searching before I may once
again enter into earth and grow toward that level of
awareness which all souls seek. I have delayed many
lifetimes that which I could have accomplished in one.
This female body in the current life has chosen not to
walk out on responsibilities and obligations, and many
debts have been paid. The time swiftly approaches
when she will be free of these debts and responsibilities that were not faced in that long ago life. She has
repaid many debts and will soon be free."

Then, the most amazing series of suggestions
came from Claire's superconscious mind. "You will
please tell Claire that she can be happy. She can and
will release the guilt and the regret that is so much a
part of her nature. You will please inform her that she
has met her debts, and she may release them and go
on in peace and trust and light. There is a life for her.
She is indeed worthy of that life. She struggles to hold
on to regret; she will not release it on her own. You
may help her by offering her the freedom to be what
she can, and to do what she can do if she will only
release the denial of worth. It would be well if you
could do this."

As those are wonderful, self-healing suggestions, I paraphrased the message back to her, as requested. I asked her to make mental pictures of the man and the village and even the scene of the "enchanted forest" so that later she could sketch the scene.

I encouraged her to keep all of the sketches. She had done this, explaining that her hand appears to draw on its own. It often draws what appears to be an Egyptian woman. She wonders if this could be a spiritual guide, or perhaps herself when she was in the Egyptian orphanage.

Claire's mercenary lifetime was not pleasant either. The pattern continued with a young man who worked and bullied his way up through the ranks in the military life.

Her Priestess incarnation appears to be her very first time upon the earth. This was in an ancient, although advanced, civilization. She had great influence through her position of leadership. People would come to her from all levels of society asking for counsel and guidance. She devoted her life to service, never having family or lover.

Claire carefully explained to me that if that Priestess lifetime came through on her first session she would not have believed it. Even now, it is too sacred for her to speak about or to share with anyone.

Her work with regression has brought understanding and an appreciation for her life. Through the years of our work she detected a number of people from the past who are present in her current life, but asked me not to include that information in this book.

2. *Case Study #2, Thomas*

In his current life, Thomas (not his real name) is a nationally known and highly respected author, researcher, teacher, and therapist. His search for certain answers in his personal life led him to explore past lives.

When we met through mutual friends, I perceived him as being highly intellectual. He seemed most willing to meet an experience of growth and to benefit from it. We have become friends and in many ways he has become a Mentor for me.

When I arrived at his home for the session, I noted that all the neighbors had well-manicured lawns while Tom had a vegetable garden surrounding his home. Also, sharing the grounds were several cats and a dog. It was obvious that he loved animals and nature. At our very first session, he attested to that with good and surprising reasons.

In his past life session, Thomas saw himself as a barefoot boy in overalls. He was standing in a pasture under the bright sun, hugging a cow. "This cow and I are feeling close. I have a bucket in my hand. I think I was supposed to be milking, but somehow I'm goofing off. There's a feeling of really being in touch with the feelings of the environment..." He and the cow were together "enjoying the atmosphere."

Later, he finds himself in a barnyard feeling sad because the cows are being taken away, along with his special cow. He feels lonely and considers running away because his cow is gone.

The next scene he pictures is the first day of a new job where he has been hired to handle cows and to upgrade production. He finds himself on a huge ranch surrounded by many cows and is drawn to one because he feels it has been hurt. As he finds a bruise on the cow and rubs it, he feels this is his gift, to be sensitive to, and to be able to communicate with, animals and to be a healer of "dumb" creatures. His devotion was moving.

When he is older, he finds himself instructing a young man, who is excited with his coaching. Later on, the young man leaves and he feels very content. He's sitting looking at the fire in the fireplace, thinking of his old cow, when he feels himself start to fade, hearing celestial music. I sense that now I'm outside in my consciousness...I'm up that hill, and my cow is with me."

When I asked what the purpose of that life was, his voice answered, "They called me a vet. They didn't know what else to call me. I found what I valued so much in terms of being in touch with nature. When I lost my cow I detached myself from that place and traveled about. I gained in that anywhere I went I felt tuned in, but I lost the one place where I was rooted. I also gained in that I could recognize others who had the same gift and help them develop it."

He said that the place was in Switzerland "with the cowbells" in 1878. He further stated another lesson that he was still in the process of learning. "There were times in that life when I sensed such a oneness with all life that it had a dreamy contentedness. That was good; but, there was a need to learn that passivity was neither necessary nor desirable to maintain that calm. When my cow was taken from me, I could have spoken up to my father and said, 'That cow I will buy from you.' Rather than accepting the merchant system as it currently operated, I could have worked to change the merchant system to make it more in accord with what I sensed from the land. I did not forge ahead with heart in the developing of new ways."

Tom's initial session was important for several reasons. First, the lessons of that life began with his love for his cow. Then, when his cow was sold, he opened himself up to a love for other animals and the ability to communicate with them. The third point is that this became the basis for his lifelong career, which he then was able to pass along to others, a tradition in European culture.

Fourthly, while still in hypnosis, he was able to give his own therapeutic evaluation of the life and of the lessons learned. He told himself how to use this information for improvement in the present. This was interesting especially in light of his training, which might be assumed to be responsible for those insights; yet, people from all walks of life and all levels of education are able to make similar evaluations by way of such meaningful and sophisticated revelations.

Several months later, I conducted Tom's second regression. When he could not focus on a pleasant memory, I tried something new in my approach. I suggested that he look at a time of sadness. This variation from my usual procedure, combined with his new familiarity with the regression process, opened a new door into his unconscious. By using the experience of the killing of a chicken, he entered a memory of a life that brought forth a powerful session.

At an earlier time in his present life, he was watching his father killing a chicken. He watched as the chicken's head bounced on the ground and its mouth moved. "....It's like I'm experiencing and feeling more than what I really know. It feels so heavy. I feel guilty. Have I seen this before? What if *my* head were chopped off? What would I see? My eyes see the blood squirting out of my own neck.

"I'm squatting on my knees and there's a man in front of me with a sword. Other people are standing around crying, and I'm pleading, no, no, don't. It's my voice they want to get rid of..they didn't like what I was saying. There had been a meeting at a long, rectangular table, and I was speaking the truth and it bothered those gathered there. I'm so upset that the truth has so little value that it can just be cut off."

"..Ugh..I'm tightening up...I'm being beheaded..I feel a sting for a second, that's all..I see my body there but I'm also everywhere..I see the world spinning around."

I deemed it appropriate to end that phase and asked where he was. He tried unsuccessfully to name a place, but kept drifting back to his insight into the event:" it's coming to me...blurting out the truth is not necessarily the way to put things right. People do what they feel they have to do."

It was time for forgiving, releasing, sending love and allowing the characters to fade. As a way of alleviating the intense emotion and tragedy of the beheading, I then suggested that he move on to a life that had the most special meaning for him. The experience that followed was unique.

"I see this beautiful courtyard garden with everything bathed in a golden light..beautiful designs with plants and flowers..much activity in the air. There seems to be an ethereal quality in that things are there, but they're not quite solid. This is our place, and there is an undercurrent of humming, like music. We have *made* this place; we *created* this reality for ourselves. The atmosphere is permeated with the presence of the vibration, the hum, the light."

"More come and appear out of the air, for we can sustain them. I am a pioneer, and this is a way-station. We have succeeded in getting something started, and now more come to join us. We are somewhere amid space, walking on some kind of ground that floats in space because *we created it.* The light is very beautiful as it leaks out from all the things we have created. It doesn't shine down, but leaks out from inside things. Everything is glowing. The light leaks out to the extent that the things are not solid."

"I am putting my hands around this T-shaped thing, pressing in the air around it to make it darker, to make it glow less, because it was just going to burst into light and cease to exist. It's a very delicate balance. It has to do with feeling..that's what's being created..a sense of feeling. It's a world that, by being of substance, there's feeling. This is apparently something new. I observe the expressions of some who come in and ooh and ah at what we have done. This is feeling. It takes something from us to do it..I sense a lapse, as though everything sort of dissolved and wasn't there for an instant, and then I focus in again, and it comes back."

"It seems important, an important stage of development. It's attracting a lot of attention. Others come to join and to experience it, and as more come, there's a greater stage which opens up. We don't quite know what to make of it or what to do, except to explore this new dimension of feeling. It's glorious to be involved in this exploration."

Later Tom referred to this experience as his very first lifetime, and recalled that it was strange, somewhat like a science fiction fantasy novel. He felt that his memory had to do with souls who were trying to create a material world and to inhabit it with created bodies as well. He added that part of the soul's discovery process was learning what *physical feeling* was like and how it enhanced our awareness.

Those three lives, and his current one was a very well-known and highly respected author of five published books, seem unrelated at first, but with deeper evaluation and study, a strong pattern emerged. Since, it is always wiser for one to discover and to evaluate one's own memories, patterns and understanding, I asked Thomas to do this.

"One of the patterns I noticed in these past life sessions is the idea of being a searcher, an explorer. Perhaps it comes sometimes from feeling lonely, or empty. Sometimes it comes from having a vision of what might be. However it comes, I am on the hunt, looking, searching. As an investigator today, the pattern holds. Being out front, the very first to arrive, making the way. There is an excitement to it, as well as a loneliness. These are themes in a couple of these regressions."

"The image of the head being cut off reminds me of a fascination today with the idea of self, or ego-consciousness, as symbolized by the head. I had a dream once where I was looking at myself in the mirror, and I had my head off and was holding it in my hands. I was amazed that I could still see without a head. Later I came across a book on Buddhism in which the author was comparing the satori experience to having no head. Exploring consciousness without a head, perhaps from the heart, is a recurrence of the theme of searching; also searching for *modes* of searching. Intellectual searching isn't everything. There's a strong emotional component to it. At first we search for love. Then we search to become love itself."

So far in this book we have worked mostly with the tool of hypnotic past-life regression for exploring deep memories. There are other methods. One such popular method is obtaining either a psychic reading or a channeled reading. Such can be valuable. But not always!

Even though one of my previous books has a large section about channeling, I feel it is ALWAYS best for people to explore THEIR OWN memories first. Our own promptings and inner guidance are more authentic and meaningful to us because of the source. A past-life reading, whether psychic, channeled or any other form, is filtered through the mind of the other person interpreting the information, and may lose in integrity thereby.

A past-life *reading* is going to ANOTHER person for information about *your* past: whether a psychic, a channel, a reader, etc. Such information can be valuable, or it can be completely off. In some cases, it can be outright fraud! There is no guarantee that another can accurately relate important information. Be especially wary of a reader who tries to tell you that you were some famous personality! Though some people were famous, most of us were normal people living in normal ways for the era. In fact, most of the famous people had the hardest lives with difficult challenges and responsibilities. And ordinary people can have extraordinary depth of wisdom.

Remember! The lesson is not WHO you were, but WHAT you learned or failed to learn. Even a good psychic can misinterpret or mis-read information. It is always wiser to go to the source, yourself, for the most important insights.

3. Case Study #3, Enrique

The following case study is of a man whom I have known for a few decades. Most of the sessions are from regressions that I guided. A few were guided by others, and two were received from psychic readings. The important point is that he received information that was pertinent and helpful to him. He did acknowledge there had been other psychic readings over the years which didn't "ring true."

The subject of this study asked to remain completely anonymous, so I'll call him Enrique. I have known him well and can witness to the fact that the lives he reported genuinely reflect his current life. He is a strange mixture of extremes and paradoxes; yet, he assured me that he DOES learn through all his unusual escapades.

I am including the entire "collection" of Enrique's past lives for a very important reason. It is to encourage *you* to do the same! It is a lot of work to gather methodically such deep memories and list them on paper, but the "final product" surely is worthwhile.

When you have a larger view of your journey

through time, you then will have a clearer picture of your destination. Our past clearly reveals our direction forward —both our patterns and our potentials.

Reading about someone else's lives may not be exciting to you. Gathering *your own* memories, and studying them, can be of utmost value. Use the example and opportunity here to encourage yourself to do the work!

The lifetimes are not in exact chronological order. They were recalled over a thirty year period. Notice the extremes of being rash and radical, as compared with being cautious and conservative, from wealth to poverty, respected to outcast, pompous to pathetic, rebellious to responsible – his own words. The whole sweeping panorama of a soul's march through time is included here.

LIFE	MALE, ancient time. The civilization was technically advanced; the architecture was beautiful.
SYNOPSIS	Probably first life on earth. Lived on large island or land mass. Student, then entered priesthood.
GAINED	Learned cooperation
LOST	Unsure
CURRENT LIFE REFLECTIONS	"My interest in the mind's potential was rooted in that life."

LIFE	MALE (several lives) in India and areas of Tibet, also one female life.

SYNOPSIS	Building temples, record keeping and recording history by carving bas-relief art; animal husbandry. People were strong and sensual.
GAINED	Happiness with life and the physical expression of living.
LOST	Spirituality overshadowed by sensuality.
CURRENT LIFE REFLECTIONS	"Since I was a small child I wanted to go to India. I eventually went, but it was a disappointment. It was not as I had 'remembered' it."

LIFE	MALE – series of lives in ancient South America and Mexico.
SYNOPSIS	Time of enlightenment and feeling very alive. Pyramids, plumage, colors, fine arts in stone and metal, study of heavens, recording history of people; keeper of records. Time of great abundance for all.
GAINED	Worked within structure to assist others.
LOST	Aloof, sense of self-importance because of position.
CURRENT LIFE REFLECTIONS	"In this present life it is very important to me not to be in any exalted position or have any title above others. Mexico and South America interests me greatly, and

I have traveled there with pleasure."

LIFE SYNOPSIS	FEMALE, India (middle period) Young woman, part of group, "kept" by a wealthy man to pro-vide entertainment..a life of gaiety and innocence. Group danced and sang/chanted to relate the legends of the people. "The Song of Rama" was an epic requiring several hours to perform. The group of young women often per-formed for those of high society.
GAINED	Close friendship of group of "sis-ters."
LOST	Pride and vanity.
CURRENT LIFE REFLECTIONS	"Once while driving I started chanting the emotional epic "RAMA," but had never heard of it previously. I could feel the emo-tions of the singer."

LIFE SYNOPSIS	FEMALE, India or nearby Unglamorous life, used and ill-kept, angry, vengeful. Hurt or killed "owner." Was killed at young age as a result of killing "owner."
GAINED	Value of freedom

LOST	Killed the person who "owned" me.
CURRENT LIFE REFLECTIONS	"I have great empathy for people who have been battered or sexually abused."

LIFE SYNOPSIS	MALE, Australia Fought with and killed chief's son. Chief's son had killed fiancee. Male was then chased, tracked, and killed.
GAINED	Understanding of justice
LOST	Personal retribution; killed a person for revenge.
CURRENT LIFE REFLECTIONS	"First regression that I experienced in the mid-1960s."

LIFE SYNOPSIS	FEMALE, Classic Greece High-class prostitute who serviced military and political leaders. Had much indirect power and influence. As a courtesan was accepted and even respected.
GAINED	Worldly influence and political intrigues
LOST	Pride in and displays of wealth and power (self-aggrandizement)
CURRENT LIFE REFLECTIONS	"This seems the only life where I had fair skin and blond hair. It was a rather laid-back life."

LIFE	FEMALE, China
SYNOPSIS	Poor, young, unwanted female who had no family. May have been mentally low-functioning; lived in a stable on the trade routes in cold mountain area. Often "used" by the mule traders, but unpaid for this service. Loved and was loved by son of a trader. Died around age 13, and body was thrown into pig pen.
GAINED	Humility; love transcends social class
LOST	Unsure
CURRENT LIFE REFLECTIONS	"Empathy for low status of women. This life seemed to be a balance to the wealth and pride of the Grecian life."

LIFE	MALE, ancient Egypt (around time of Moses)
SYNOPSIS	High priest or advisor to the ruler. As result, he had much power which was used to help his friends and the priests. Did nothing to help others although much could have been done. In some cases, took power away from others.
GAINED	Comfortable with wealth and power.

LOST	Abuse of power and failure to assist others.
CURRENT LIFE REFLECTIONS	"This life is being balanced now in the present. I empower others, while having no power myself. My trip to Egypt was a disappointment compared to the grandeur of that ancient time."

LIFE	MALE, desert life
SYNOPSIS	Boy carrying water to the slaves. Dry climate, digging for water in hot sands, high winds. Had little food and crude clothing.
GAINED	Learned simple things have great value; learned by listening carefully.
LOST	Bitterness, futility.
CURRENT LIFE REFLECTIONS	"Fortunately that was a short life."

LIFE	MALE, Phoenician trader, member group of vagabonds
SYNOPSIS	A life spent mostly "on the seas," trading at many ports. Often cheated and stole from others.
GAINED	Enjoyment in travel, adventure, learning new places and meeting new people.
LOST	Crude and without ethics

CURRENT LIFE REFLECTIONS	"Life has brought me back to the same areas dozens of times."

LIFE SYNOPSIS	MALE, "on the seas" Traveling on the Mediterranean Sea when a sudden storm arose, and the young male was drowned.
GAINED	?
LOST	?
CURRENT LIFE REFLECTIONS	"Perhaps a balance for attacking ships where others were drowned. I do not like ships or boats, and I am still a poor swimmer. I almost drowned as a teenager."

LIFE SYNOPSIS	MALE, French, Crusades Lived in a village with wife and children. Went on the Crusades in hope of gaining riches and glory; but instead met with disaster, betrayal, and death.
GAINED	Learned the foolishness of war and aggression.
LOST	Lost family, wife, and life in the search for material gain.
CURRENT LIFE REFLECTIONS	"A terrible loss!"

LIFE	MALE, Persia (on trade routes from Europe to Mid-East)

SYNOPSIS	Lived in a small town on trade routes and traded with travelers. Prospered from the travelers, but eventually a Crusades army came through, and they destroyed and killed all in their path. Dance was the greatest pleasure in life, and family was close and helpful.
GAINED	Good marriage and family, productive work making pottery.
LOST	Unwilling to heed advice/warning from others to flee the oncoming Crusaders.
CURRENT LIFE REFLECTIONS	"My wife in that lifetime is my wife now. She still likes to dance; I do not."

LIFE SYNOPSIS	MALE, South Seas From Europe – "sabbatical life." Jumped ship somewhere in Polynesia. Married an island maiden. Enjoyed life of simple pleasures in a society of happy people. Learned their dance and customs. A time of happiness and innocence.
GAINED	Adapted to new people and customs.
LOST	Nothing seemed to come up.
CURRENT LIFE REFLECTIONS	"Since childhood, I have loved and continue to enjoy Polynesian music and culture."

LIFE	MALE, American Indian (maybe in more than one life)
SYNOPSIS	Old man with a minor position as an elder. Realized their way of life was dying; the people were dying. Chanted funeral dirge.
GAINED	Resigned to the inevitable.
LOST	Sadness and despair for what once was.
CURRENT LIFE REFLECTIONS	"I have great interest in and respect for the American Indians."

LIFE	MALE, Caribbean area, privateers/pirate
SYNOPSIS	Chose to rob as a career/way of life; a member of a group of looters seeking plunder. However, this group was not typically bloodthirsty. An accepted and often politically sanctioned way of life at the time. Died in early 20's of a sexual disease.
GAINED	Travel, free lifestyle
LOST	A wasted life with a predilection to rum, loose women, and disease.
CURRENT LIFE REFLECTIONS	"I sure hope that's out of my system!"

LIFE	MALE, Himalayas (India, the Foothills)
SYNOPSIS	Unwanted; or his parents died in the early part of his life. From the village in which he lived, he could see the grand mountains. When in his early teens, he went to the mountains to live..mostly alone. When travelers came, however, he shared his shelter and food with them.
GAINED	Helping others, contemplation, survival.
LOST	Hiding/running away rather than facing feelings of being unwanted/unloved.
CURRENT LIFE REFLECTIONS	"Good fortune has always come to me through travel. I truly believe that is because I helped travelers in the Himalayas lifetime (and maybe in other lives also.)"

LIFE	MALE (3 different but sequential lives) ROME (around the time of Christ)
SYNOPSIS	In two lives (one as a Zealot and one as a Pharisee) the males were outspoken and violently against the Roman empire. The third lifetime as a citizen who worked on wagons delivering goods and sup-

	plies for the army. Often stole supplies and sold them for "favors" or other payments.
GAINED	Courage to question those in authority, and understanding life from another's position.
LOST	Too outspoken and silenced by being killed. Stealing.
CURRENT LIFE REFLECTIONS	"Business often takes me near Roman ruins. The Roman period interests me."

LIFE SYNOPSIS	MALE, Austria
	Catholic priest with a small parish. Lived a simple life with kind people whom he knew for many years.
GAINED	Service and humility.
LOST	Lonely without a companion; dogmatic and self-righteous.
CURRENT LIFE REFLECTIONS	"It would have been a good life except for the celibacy."

LIFE SYNOPSIS	MALE, Ireland
	Catholic priest who was not kind. An alcoholic.
GAINED	Service to others.
LOST	Ritualized and cold. Hatred for the English, alcoholism.
CURRENT LIFE REFLECTIONS	"I still dislike British pomposity and arrogance."

Enrique was encouraged to find patterns from this incredible spread of lives. He took the difficult patterns first:

"I often ran away or denied my family and friends. In a number of lives, I was not married and lived alone. I avoided populated places. Worst of all I abandoned my family for gain through war. In other times I, myself, was abandoned.

"Perhaps my biggest example of denial was the alcoholism in at least two lives: the Irish priest and the privateer in the Caribbean."

"As I studied the patterns of my lives, the strongest negative pattern seems to be the way I go to such extremes. I have had lives at the very highest, and again, at the very lowest levels of society. A few lifetimes were exalted with wealth and power; yet, a few balanced that with poverty and absolutely no power or influence."

"Sexuality was also a stumbling-block for my spiritual growth. There were some lifetimes of complete sexual indulgences, and then lives balanced with complete celibacy. I probably perpetrated wrong as much as I was subsequently wronged. More male lives than female ones."

"I also had to admit that I stole as a way of life several times. I've robbed and been robbed. Perhaps I liked the excitement of that kind of life, but I re-ran it too much. I also re-ran dying young and sometimes violently."

Enrique was also encouraged to discover the POSITIVE patterns in his past, and he did a very creditable job of it.

"In a few lifetimes I worked with stone, metals,

and pottery. Travel is a big theme from my past and continues to be in the current life."

"Dancing was important in the past, but not currently. Often I recorded history and preserved traditions in various manners. Religious and spiritual purposes are a definite pattern, both then and at the present time."

"As I think about the various aspects of myself, the other lives and their parts of my deeper self, I find that there is one person whom I truly admire and feel the strongest respect and love toward – the little Chinese waif who lived in a stable. She had absolutely nothing going for her. Most of her life was on the brink of starvation. She scraped out the manure from the shed and enclosures where the animals were kept; yet, in and throughout that entire lifetime, she never complained, finding moments of true happiness."

"The lifetime that I believe I am trying to heal or balance at the present time is the Egyptian one where I had great power and did nothing useful with it. During my current life I have had no power, or even the persuasion for it, and strive at all times to be of use to others."

B. To Live Life More Fully, Study Life

In those three case studies we have been given a legacy: the identifying, balancing, and healing of patterns of the past. We have perceived the inner-workings of three souls. This careful examination of the past lives of three people is less an intellectual pursuit than it is a preview for opening ourselves to our greater purpose, using God's Magnificent Plan for

Humanity.

"Earth School" is a life-long quest for learning and discovery. For some, it is an intellectual or philosophical pursuit. For others, it is a hands-on, experiential adventure of doing. I advocate the action approach: to learn through teaching, to experience through doing, to LIVE with passion and purpose.

Reading is wonderful; it opens new doors and reveals new vistas. But the best learning comes through experience – and complete immersion. Immersion is *involvement* and *activity*.

For instance, if you should want to learn about government or politics, the best way to learn is, obviously, in the "doing" of politics or government. Taking courses in those subjects may help in understanding the historical aspects of government or with the study of party platforms, but the real learning and revelations will come in and through an involvement in the political arena itself.

Similarly, when we wish to learn the joy of contemplation, we must first find a place for that pursuit. It could be in our own home or on a distant mountain top. The place is much less important than the act of our going and entering into a state of silence.

If you wish to learn about love – in depth – you must find someone or something to love. Then you learn and grow in and through that love. Books may help, classes may improve your sensitivity to love, but the *experience* is of the greatest value. Immersion is the key.

**How many faces of lives past can you
find in this Tree of Life?**

Artist: Kathye Mendes

C. Hate is a Spiritual Disease

Even negative emotions or patterns are learned best and understood through immersion. Should you wish to learn the dynamics of anger or hatred, visit those places or those people who are immersed in such behavior. We must *learn* not to become angry, not to become hateful, but instead to be aware of those traps and find ways of helping to free people from such emotions, and to eliminate the destructive patterns which hold them captive.

We will not heal the world of hatred if we fear it, or simply banish those people infected with it. ALL negative behavior must be faced. Ultimately, we must search also within ourselves. Some are quite eager to accuse others of anger or hatred, but are most reluctant to look into their own troubled or critical hearts.

For example, a woman, whom I respect, had a problem dealing with death. She had lost her father, her mother, and her grandfather (who had become her guardian at a very young age). She felt betrayed, hurt, and angry with death. For many years she went from counselor to counselor, and therapist to therapist, with little help or benefit. She felt that she had been robbed of a family's love, and was angry at "death" for wounding her.

In desperation, and in an attempt at self-healing, she decided to join the Hospice movement. She trained to be a Hospice volunteer and was given people to visit and families to help who were experiencing – or were soon to experience – death. She helped them, and they helped her.

Soon she began to realize that God had not punished her, that she was not singled out for tragedy. She realized that EVERYONE dies, or will die, as a natural progression of life. She loved her patients and, in the healing work, began to heal her own life and to alleviate the fear and anger that preyed upon her own psyche. I have the greatest admiration for this woman, for her willingness to confront her deepest angers and fears, to learn the lesson of understanding, and to heal her life accordingly.

This lesson is plain for everyone. Work to confront your worst fears, soothe your angers, extinguish your seething hatred, destroy your demanding little demons. Not in theory, not intellectually, but in the doing of wise and productive activities. Don't struggle with the symptoms; that path could last forever – figuratively and literally! Go to the *source* of the patterns. HEAL the past. LEARN your soul lessons. Forgive others.

D. Forgiveness

My introduction to the overwhelming importance of forgiveness is an outgrowth of my research into past-lives, which started when I was in high school. At that time, I probably would have said that any career as a hypnotherapist and past-life explorer could come about only by accident. After three decades of research, I believe that few pivotal events in life are accidental. Rather, they are the result of the exercise of one's free will, under the guidance of one's subconscious or inner mind -- all working together to choose a particular path when one reaches a crossroad in life.

The pivotal event in my life came when my brother

purchased a used book for five cents. That nickel, that book entitled *The Search for Bridey Murphey* by Morey Bernstein, changed my life forever. It initiated the career which gradually has become a mission, one that I have followed for more than thirty years. My experience during that time has convinced me that we are eternal beings, or souls, who are given the opportunity to return to a physical life on Earth countless times to attend the "Earth School" for our spiritual development.

Why are we granted more than one life? I believe that for more than any other reason, it is *to learn the lessons of forgiveness*. Almost everyone claims to forgive others; but in reality, few of us do so. People say one thing and often do quite the contrary. But the many experiences and lessons learned in previous lifetimes enable us to forgive much more easily.

Forgiveness is both a modern and an ancient tool. It's a powerful method for healing our hurts and painful memories. Although forgiveness is often associated with religious work, it is far more vast; it encompasses the entire field of spirituality. To my mind, the word "religious" pertains to the beliefs and doctrines of specific faith traditions. On the other hand, "Spiritual" is all-inclusive and relates to the fullness of life — the Creative Forces or Life Force everywhere.

To return to my own early awareness of the theory of reincarnation: with only minimal training at first, I immediately began attempting either to duplicate or to disprove the Bridey Murphey experiment of past-life recall. The process involved hypnosis in order to access deep, soul memories. I had absolutely no idea where those experiments would lead me. Although at the time I was a student (in the familiar sense of the word), I began to realize that life itself was like a much larger school. My early research with hypnosis revealed a form or level of schooling that reached higher than the traditional, mainstream curriculum which I had been studying. I was finding now a more vast and more advanced school of life that had always been going on all around me! Earth School is a grand institution wherein we can learn various lessons, be given many tests, and specialize in different subjects.

Failure to forgive can be likened to a form of spiritual cancer that eats away at the spirit. Some past-life researchers and spiritual philosophers even suggest that a lack of forgiveness can develop into physical and mental illness. Even though I've received considerable training as a hypnotherapist, my work has been conducted from a non-medical background; therefore, I don't feel qualified to agree or disagree with that issue. I *can* say, however, that forgiveness work is a win/win endeavor. There is healing and benefit to be gained and absolutely nothing to lose in forgiving ourselves and others.

An even more astounding discovery from my years of research is that often the very same souls (in different incarnations) continue to repeat and to re-run the same scenarios in new settings. The countries may switch, the calendars may change, but the basic *issues* remain the same. Work with my clients has revealed deeper causal events to the experiences we later reap: as we have all been admonished in the Bible, "As you sow, so shall you reap." We plant seeds and their results are later to be harvested, even though we have forgotten what we planted, or when, or where.

**FORGIVENESS IS THE KEY TO OPEN
YOUR HEART'S MEMORIES
Artist: Kathye Mendes**

A key principle in past-life research is the identification of repeated or recurring events — what we call "patterns" — an expression that was often used in the Cayce readings. **Forgiveness work usually begins with recognizing those patterns** because they reveal the areas of difficulty. This is an effort that requires personal honesty and courage.

For most souls, the most frequent method of forgiveness has been denial. People tend to react negatively to events. They often deny the problem rather than forgive. Such reactions usually lead to retaliation which leads, in turn, to revenge. And so, the cyclic pattern can go on and on. Forgiveness is the golden principle that can *break* the pattern.

As I've found with some of my clients, even death

does not end a pattern of vengeance and hatred. Hypnotic sessions can reveal centuries-old series of events. Without forgiveness, an action would lead to revenge, and revenge would inflict more hurt. The hurt, in turn, would lead to retaliation, then to more hurt, in a vicious cycle.

An approach to break this cycle is to ask the hypnotized persons what *they* can do to release the hurt. (Actually, it's a question one can ask one's self about a problem area, even without hypnosis). In my sessions I find that the clients' higher guidance instructs them in better ways of response. Merely re-playing the hurt is like rubbing salt on an open wound. But forgiveness exercises are like a soothing salve or ointment to heal ancient wounds.

In fact, true forgiveness is more comprehensive than just letting go and releasing the hurt or seeming injustice. Forgiveness entails an analysis of the situation in order to avoid similar circumstances in the future. Most of all, it is an opportunity to *learn and to grow* through life's experiences. Often Earth School's hardest lessons bestow the greatest rewards.

The following story illustrates some of my points: A woman in her late 50's came to my office, interested in some hypnotic regression work because of her depression. In our first session, I followed my standard procedure to guide my client into deep hypnosis, and we first did a present life regression. Already she was beginning to feel that there had been a tragedy, that something very bad had happened. But it wasn't until we got into past-life material that the details became evident.

As is my usual technique, I suggested to her, as

she moved back into a past-life, that she first look down at her feet. She reported that she was wearing button-up shoes that were heeled and either dark brown or maybe black. Then, when I asked her to describe the rest of her attire, she said that she was wearing a flowered dress which was gathered with a belt tied in the back. It had a button-down bodice with a lace collar and cuffs.

Next my client began to describe various aspects of her life, and a few of her memories from childhood. She lived in a small, secluded community and was part of the church choir. After relating this sort of image from this past-life, she seemed to home in on very significant events. There had been an awful tragedy: the young man she loved had been killed in an accident or in a war. She never got over the loss of him, stating emphatically, "I could never love again."

Still in deep hypnosis, she continued with her account. Time passed and her parents wanted her to marry another man. Her mother thought it would be a good idea, and her father would have been very angry if she had refused. Reluctantly, she agreed, thinking that maybe she couldn't keep on loving a dead person all her life. But they had had so many dreams, and she had loved him so deeply, that moving ahead with this marriage was very difficult.

Next she saw and described the scenes surrounding her wedding. Many people in the town were very busy, sewing, cooking, and planning for the wedding. "Everyone is so excited except me. I'm going through with it because I don't want to hurt my mother and the man I'm going to marry." Then she described the marriage ceremony itself, which was in this little country church and conducted by a preacher who came by only two or three times per year. Afterward, she and her new husband departed, going off to spend the night close-by because he didn't have a lot of money for something like a honeymoon. They are in a horse-drawn carriage. "I feel more for the horse than I do for my husband."

Then she seemed to move to the end of that lifetime, and she reminisced: "It's been a hard life. We farmed. I lost several babies but we have four children: three boys and a beautiful daughter, who after growing up had two children of her own. As hard as I tried to love my husband, I couldn't. At times we were almost like two strangers in the house."

Finally, near the end of the hypnosis session, we did some healing work. I asked what she could do to alleviate the depression that seemed to have carried over into the current lifetime. She responded, "I'm still looking for that perfect person whom I loved. Maybe instead of trying to overcome the grief, I should let myself grieve. My emotions were too deep. I felt too deeply and when he was lost, I couldn't get away from it."

I asked what tasks she could give herself to help heal. "If I keep myself mentally busy it helps. To concentrate on helping other people and not on myself."

Then we turned to the forgiveness exercise, and it turned out to be one of the longest I ever had with a client. The exercise was for her to send love from her eyes to the eyes of the people in that past-life. She immediately did well with everyone except the young man who was killed and lost to her. She cried profusely. She would not or could not let him go.

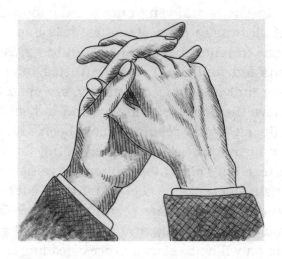

Forgiveness

EXPERIENCE AN ULTIMATE PURPOSE
Artist: Jeffrey Winchester

Finally, after a long time, I asked her to talk to that man. A few moments later, she said, "He wants to go." Upon realizing that, she was able to bless him and to release him.

When I brought her back to normal waking consciousness and the session ended, she seemed like a different person. In fact, I saw her again three weeks later. She looked so much happier, and said that it was as if a giant weight had been removed.

Of course, it's not just individuals like this woman who struggle with lessons of forgiveness. Entire *groups* of people — for example, religious groups or entire nations — must learn the greater lessons of forgiveness. Reactions and vengeance are the most destructive of all human characteristics. It is important for everyone to remember to forgive, and to preserve the *lessons learned*. Vast opportunities for healing, whether individually or collectively, are open to those who have the courage to forgive and to heal.

Edgar Cayce's readings have been an on-going source of inspiration to me regarding forgiveness. Those teachings offer humanity much valuable insight and instruction of this topic, and their counsel was, **Condemn no one**. The readings also explained a method for individuals and groups to find common ground on which to start a process leading to forgiveness. Here was Cayce's advice: Magnify the agreements and minimize the differences; magnify the virtues and minimize the faults. In essence, this means to search actively for the good in others while downplaying the shortcomings.

How can you recognize people who are mired in anger or vengeance? Some are very easy to spot because of their words: "I'll never forgive him," or, "I'll never forgive the way she hurt me." Those are obvious messages!

Yet, many other people hold on to destructive anger by subtly masking it. Sometimes it's expressed as a type of passive aggression. Such people may, on the surface, appear to do good, but they actually devote considerable time to reaction and to retaliation. One example comes quickly to mind: people who say that they believe in God yet spend most of their time discussing evil. Such individuals tend to become preoccupied with the devil rather than talking about and demonstrating the love of God for all humanity.

Forgiveness exercises, like other forms of exercise, should start slowly and carefully. As strength and confidence build, bigger and bigger issues can be forgiven. As in all of the Earth School's lessons, find the middle path between foolish optimism and pathetic pessimism. The unrealistic optimist hopes that forgiveness will happen without effort; the dreary pessimist fears it will never come. Forgiveness comes with realistic approaches and practical solutions based on one's personal situation (or a group's situation). Past-life exploration procedures are a proven, practical approach. Positive re-programming through hypnotherapy is becoming more and more widely applied and accepted.

But past-life exploration can come through other means, too — for example, dreams, meditation, and visions. Here is a story about one of my own forgiveness experiences linked to a past-life recall that came as a vision. It directly concerned my need for self-forgiveness and the problem that I had often faced in the current lifetime regarding intimate relationships.

In the mid-1960's I was living in a remote part of Spain, where I had gone to escape the bitter New England winter. Ironically, the house where I lived was made of stone and was unheated, as are most in that part of Spain. I was not much warmer that winter than I would have been at home. In addition, I was full of sadness over a failed relationship and the loss of a son (from the relationship) who had gone with his mother. I brooded over other unsatisfactory relationships too, for I saw the beginnings of my pattern of difficulties.

For several days, off and on, I prayed and

meditated, hoping for insight into the origins of my problems.

One day I sat drearily in my room, sick with the flu and a high fever. In my fevered state, a waking dream, or vision, came with very strong images and powerful feelings of sadness and tragedy. I was in a past-life, in France, and I was abandoning a wife and our three children, two of whom had been born and one I didn't yet realize had been conceived. By the standards of the day, it was a good life — I had work; we had food. It was a normal peasant's life. And I was leaving that good life to go on one of the Crusades.

In that vision, I saw that I left my wife for the magic, the joy, the glamour, and the glory of the Crusade — and for the lure of riches. My comrades and I were going out to fight the infidel for Christ, and we thought it was going to be great fun. We were fools! They called the Crusade holy; for me it was hell. We marched, and we marched, and we marched. When I got to Jerusalem, to the very sight of the Holy City, I died on the side of the road. I died of disease and exhaustion. My body fell into the ditch. The Crusader army kept marching.

That was the vision. It provided me with physical and emotional release and the opportunity to forgive myself. I cried; it seemed as though I cried for hours. When I finally dried my eyes, I was filled with peace and self-acceptance. I was grateful that my prayer for insight had been answered. In my mind, I sent my French wife my profound regret for abandoning her and our children.

I did not know what to do with the information I now had. But at the time, it was enough that I had information that shed light on my state of mind, that my pain had been relieved, that I experienced calm, self-acceptance, and most importantly, *self-forgiveness*. Nor did I feel a need to do anything. I simply resumed my life. When I recovered from the fever, I traveled throughout Spain and six months later returned to America. But my vision and its stimulus to a healing self-forgiveness stayed with me. In retrospect, it is a key episode in my life.

There are numerous effective techniques for bringing and for building upon forgiveness. With my hypnotherapy clients, whenever possible, I like to include visual, auditory, *and* kinesthetic approaches so that a person can work with all levels of response. As I describe them, consider how you could also make use of them via self-hypnosis, meditative imagery, or prayer.

For those who are primarily visually oriented, I emphasize a technique in which they look into the eyes of the person who hurt them or whom they hurt. Then I ask my clients, as best they can, to send love and forgiveness from their own eyes to the eyes of the other person, to send their forgiveness and blessing. Then I give instructions to let that individual fade from view. Since for some people this process takes only a few seconds and for many others it takes several minutes, I will say, "There is no rush for you to do this, take all the time you wish. When you are ready, just tell me, and we will continue."

To be attentive to the auditory level, I might ask the clients to hold an imaginary verbal dialogue with the person involved. Depending on the situation, my guidance will sound something like this: "Now put into words and speak aloud what you really want to say to that person. Say whatever it is that comes to you. Just begin when you are ready." Through the forgiveness perspective of time and experience, sometimes I also ask the client to express aloud what they think the other person would communicate.

To engage the kinesthetic process, I ask what specific tasks the clients could do in the *current* life to help heal or balance the memory. I also ask for descriptions of their own feelings *and* the feelings of the other person involved. Those emotional episodes are healing in themselves, and the tasks they give themselves are usually realistic and later prove to be effective.

Although many clients work best with just one or two of those three processes, some people can forgive best by working at all three levels — visual, auditory, and kinesthetic.

One warning, however, comes with the discovery of just how powerful and reliable forgiveness exercises can be. We should never harm or hurt someone, thinking in the back of our minds that later we can always clean things up with forgiveness techniques.

Earth School is a continuing educational program of practicing the Golden Rule to "Do unto others...." But don't expect everyone to have learned the healing lessons of forgiveness. Each soul, however, *will* learn it with time.

And for those who are parents, there is a special opportunity to teach sincere forgiveness to their children while they are still young. Probably it will be the *most valuable lesson* that parents ever impart — in addition to learning it more deeply for themselves at the same time!

The two most important principles for all humanity are right at the heart of forgiveness:

*Love every person as you would love yourself.

*Treat others as you would have them treat you.

Treat others, *all* others, humanely. If everyone would abide by those ideals, there would be no need for forgiveness because there would be nothing to forgive.

Chapter XII

Healing the Present

A. Growth Occurs in Resolving Problems

et's review what we've learned. Each of us has had situations that seem to repeat themselves over and over in our lifetimes. Those experiences seem to be trying to teach us something. We have created patterns in our lives to teach us lessons, and by understanding that, we can more easily recognize the pattern and work through it to learn the lesson.

A pattern will repeat itself until there is a break placed in its path to stop the repetition. The break comes with the realization that the pattern exists and the taking of action to stop it. We all can find the strength inside to recognize that patterns exist in our lives. Once we accept that and find the pattern, and have the desire and courage to make the changes, we can break that pattern.

One way to determine where a pattern exists would be to write down all that you can about troubled areas in your life. Write down everything you can remember about the situation - feelings, things that were said, people involved, and so on. Those situations could be relationships, jobs, friends, places you have lived, etc. Any area that is troublesome for you probably has a pattern rooted in it.

Once you have written everything you can think of that is related to the situation, examine all that you have. Remove yourself from the situation and look at the big picture, read between the lines of what you have written, listen to your Self, and trust your inner guidance. Soon, you will see the pattern appear before you. All of the pieces of the puzzle will begin to fit together.

Now that you have determined that a pattern exists and that you want to change it, you take the steps to decide how to go about doing it. First, look within yourself and realize that you are worth the time and effort it may take to make that change. Change seems to be difficult for people to accept; however, change is necessary for growth. Work through all of the details you have written down so that you have a full understanding of what you have been doing in the past. Ask yourself how that pattern has served you, what you needed from the situation, and what it provided for you? Then, decide what you are going to do to make those changes for the better. What steps are you going to take to achieve the goal of breaking that pattern? Understand that you don't need that pattern anymore. This is a process of healing that will take place within you and is a great gift you can give yourself.

Patterns do not always exist in a negative sense. You have positive patterns as well. You must also recognize their existence and utilize them to their fullest. Don't let them go unnoticed or fall by the wayside while you try to work with negative patterns. The positive repetitions that occur can be very beneficial and uplifting, so use them.

All of us can learn so much about ourselves by examining the details of our lives. We can recognize the good areas and the areas where we need to do some work. Your life is an ongoing lesson. You are always being given situations to help you to learn, to grow, and to advance. Take the ball and run with it. Don't see your experiences as hard luck or life dealing you a bad hand. Learn and grow through recognition, acceptance, and change. That is why you have been provided with those situations — for your growth.

B. A Present Life Pattern

As I look back at my own experiences with patterns, an event comes to mind that had tremendous impact on my life. It was a turning point for me in understanding and in working with patterns. This is a present life pattern — a revelation I shall always remember.

After traveling abroad for a couple of months, I returned home to a less than perfect situation. My love of four years had found another man. With nowhere else to go, I decided to visit an old friend. While I was there, I was asked to speak with my friend's sister's new boyfriend. I will refer to them as Pete and Jenny. Apparently, their relationship was not taking off as was hoped and my friend thought that I could help in some way. In my state of mind, I was not sure how much help I could be, but I thought I should at least try.

I met Pete and for lack of anything to discuss, I

asked about his astrological sign. Little did I realize the door that was opening for myself, Pete, and others. He told me that he was a Taurus and that Jenny was a Sagittarius. The conversation progressed and Pete explained that several of his previous relationships had been with Sagittarians. He continued by telling me that Jenny was a triple Sagittarian. This means her sun, moon, and rising sign are all in the sign of Sagittarius.

Having some background in astrology, by no means a professional astrologer, I immediately realized that Jenny must be a free spirit. Sagittarians tend to carry the motto of "don't fence me in." On the other hand, Pete — being a Taurus — most likely wanted a strong and steady lifestyle including marriage, children, and a nice home.

Pete went on to explain that Jenny does not want to get into a serious relationship or ever get married, have children, or any responsibilities. This, of course, is just the opposite of what Pete would like. As long as there was no commitment involved, Jenny was fun-loving, carefree, and exuberant — all qualities that Pete loved because he lacked them.

Pete began to see that this was exactly the same problem he had with other women he dated. At that point an inspiration came to me to chart his previous relationships, their astrological data, if known, and the reason for their breakup. We examined past situations and compared the differences and similarities. Our final step was to write everything down so that we could analyze and evaluate it. Each step flowed naturally into the next. Each piece of the puzzle fit into its proper place as Pete's pattern began to unfold in front of us.

The evidence was strong, Pete had a pattern of dating Sagittarian women who were fun and attractive but definitely not ready for marriage. In an effort to help, I suggested that Pete date women who were not Sagittarian.

I decided that I should do the same exercise for myself. I made time to list my previous relationships and their sun, moon, and rising signs, when they were known. From my analysis, a clear pattern evolved. I too had been attracted to women of a certain astrological sign. This made sense because my pattern in relationships was definitely predictable. At that point, I decided to take my own advice and to carefully choose a better match.

In Pete's case, Sagittarian women were not the problem. The real problem was that they were not a good combination for him. That is the key. It was Pete's pattern only. It does not apply to other people under the sign of Taurus and Sagittarius who may get together. Every person is different and every person has a separate set of patterns.

As a follow-up to Pete's case, I saw him two years after we had done our analysis of his pattern. He was happily married to a woman of the Libra sign. They were expecting their first child. So as you can see, by recognizing the pattern and changing it, you can overcome the pattern you have established.

My work with this case was a great learning experience. By following a process of sharing, talking and analyzing, we managed to find the pattern and to determine what kind of a change needed to be made. Each of us is capable of doing this in our own lives.

We must be strong enough to admit that we have patterns that exist in our lives and then be willing to change or work with them to create a better person.

C. Your Homework: Worksheets

"Healing the Present" is a polite way of saying that now it is time to get to work in a new way, using new tools for betterment. This chapter is your home work - literally and figuratively - a meaningful self-study in the privacy and comfort of your home, or in your spiritual sanctuary.

The following lists of questions will help you to think about your life. In answering questions and then analyzing the responses, you will gain valuable insights. Nobody else can do this for you; it is *self-directed* learning.

You may answer the questions by writing directly in this book or, better still, you may begin a journal or a diary in order to have privacy and plenty of room to write as much as you want. Deep, self-honesty and a desire to grow will give you a clear and self-revealing picture of yourself - for YOU. This is also an exercise in self-healing and personal growth. Remember, no one else need see your answers unless you wish to share them.

If you choose to write in a separate journal, be sure to write the questions as well as the answers. Then, when you re-read the material years from now, you will still have the questions as well as your answers.

Take your time in answering the questions; this is a *valuable use* of the time in your life and it will even help you in designing your next life! We are just as responsible for our future lives as we are for our current one!

Be candid and honest in your answers; write from your heart more than from your mind. Temporarily, put ego and logic aside and allow the answers to come from your inner guidance.

It could be fun to do the exercises in the comfort of your Spiritual Sanctuary, but that is not necessary. What is important is to DO the work.

WORKSHEET 1

1. List ten people (living or dead) whom you would
   like to meet:

   1. _____   6. _____
   2. _____   7. _____
   3. _____   8. _____
   4. _____   9. _____
   5. _____   10. _____

2. In what areas of life did they become well known?
   (authors, political leaders, religious leaders, artists,
   performers, etc.)_____

   _____

3. In what ways do they contribute to humanity?

   _____

4. Were their lives easy or challenging? _____

   _____

5. What are the similarities among those people?

   _____

6. What are their differences? _____

   _____

WORKSHEET 1 (continued)

7. In general, what are their strengths and weaknesses? _____

   _____

8. What other patterns can you discover in this list of
   people? _____

   _____

WORKSHEET 2

Positive Patterns of a Friend or Loved One

Please answer the following questions regarding a special friend or loved one in order to help to identify positive patterns in that person's life:

What is that person doing that is working well? ____

_____

What are that person's talents? _____

_____

What is unique about that person? _____

_____

What does that person do so well that you can't resist telling others? _____

_____

Your Own Positive Patterns
(Answer the same questions about yourself)

What are you doing that is working well? _____

_____

What are your talents? _____

_____

What is unique about you? _____

_____

What do you do so well that people can't resist telling others? _____

WORKSHEET 3

List four important teachers or mentors in your life who are *not* in an educational field. How and what did they teach you? What, regarding their role in your life, are you most grateful for?

1.

2.

3.

4.

What similarities or patterns can you discover in the above?

WORKSHEET 4

List five people for whom you served as a teacher or mentor:

1.

2.

3.

4.

5.

What did you teach, and how? (That is, did you speak, demonstrate, instruct, etc.?)

What similarities did those people have? Do they remember you as a teacher, or do they not?

WORKSHEET 5

List twelve things that you would most love to do:

1. _____   7. _____

2. _____   8. _____

3. _____   9. _____

4. _____   10. _____

5. _____   11. _____

6. _____   12. _____

Now, study this list to detect any patterns or themes. For example, do the activities take place mostly indoors or outdoors? Are they predominantly things to be done alone or with other people? Do they cost money, or are they, basically, free? What patterns could other people find in this list? Please write your answers below.

WORKSHEET 6

Before reading any further, please list seven words that are most important or meaningful to you:

1. _____   5. _____

2. _____   6. _____

3. _____   7. _____

4. _____

What are those words about? Can you detect any similarities or links between then?

   Kahlil Gibran once said, "We shall never understand one another until the language is reduced to seven words." Barbara Young wrote the following in her book, *This Man From Lebanon - A Study of Kahlil Gibran:** "We were pausing after a longish period of work and entirely without preliminary the poet asked, 'Suppose you were compelled to give up - to forget, all the words you now have except seven - what are the seven words that you would keep?' With very little hesitation I chose the words 'God, life, love, beauty, Earth' - and then I could not find the two more words to make seven. So I said, 'Tell me what your words would be.'

---

*Alfred A. Knopf, Publishers, New York City, 1945.

'You have forgotten the most important words of all,' he said, 'without which the rest are impotent.' That amazed me - but he went on. 'The two most important words are *you* and *I* - without those two there would need be no others. *We must be* and *we must take.*' Then he spoke slowly and almost breathlessly, 'These are my seven words: You, I, take, God, love, beauty, earth.'"

A Personal Note from the Author

While we are working with those favorite or meaningful words, I will share my own personal list:

1. Adventure   (of all sorts - travel, spiritual, even trance adventures)
2. Generosity   (to give more and do more than expected)
3. Work   (creating, building, helping)
4. Humor   (a valuable gift for everyone; it's free and it's fun)
5. Thankfulness   (sincere appreciation of life's blessings)
6. Balance   (vital for all Libras!)
7. Service   (through service comes our greatest fulfillment)

WORKSHEET 7

Write about *your strengths* in the following areas:*

1. Personal appearance _____
2. Finances - resources _____
3. Communications _____
4. Home - residence _____
5. Pleasure - sports _____
6. Health _____
7. Relationships - Romance _____
8. Psychic matters _____
9. Education - travel _____
10. Career - reputation _____
11. Friendships - groups _____
12. Unconscious or spiritual matters _____

How do you use or apply these gifts most effectively:

1. Personal appearance _____
2. Finances - resources _____
3. Communications _____
4. Home - residence _____
5. Pleasure - sports _____
6. Health _____
7. Relationships - Romance _____
8. Psychic matters _____
9. Education - travel _____
10. Career - reputation _____
11. Friendships - groups _____
12. Unconscious or spiritual matters _____

*Topic order is based upon the "Houses" of an astrological chart. Compare your answers to the activity or planets in the respective houses, using your natal or "birth" chart.

WORKSHEET 8

If you were asked to house-sit a friend's mountain cabin for two weeks, which ten books would you most want to take?

1. _____   6. _____
2. _____   7. _____
3. _____   8. _____
4. _____   9. _____
5. _____   10. _____

What do these books have in common? What is their genre or subject matter? Are they entertaining, or are they educational?

What were the five most influential books in your life, and why?

1. _____   4. _____
2. _____   5. _____
3. _____

List the five most influential movies of your life. Why did they influence you?

1. _____   4. _____
2. _____   5. _____
3. _____

Again, what are the themes and patterns found in these materials?

WORKSHEET 9

And now, a few random questions:

1. What is the *greatest truth* that you are aware of?

2. If you could attend tuition-free any school or university and take any course(s), what would you study? Why?

3. If you could travel with all expenses paid, which *seven* countries would you visit first?

4. To which countries would you *not* want to go?

5. What patterns can you observe here?

WORKSHEET 10

Write a paragraph describing an exceptional experience in your current life:

Describe another exceptional event:

Now describe a third significant time:

And finally, a fourth and important episode:

What are the similarities in these experiences? The differences? Did they involve other people and if so, in what manner?

WORKSHEET 11

Negative Patterns

What do you detest or hate more than anything?

What else do you really dislike?

When do you feel gut-level revulsion?

What are your three worst fears?

List *five* of the hardest things you have ever had to do in your current life:

1. _____   4. _____
2. _____   5. _____
3. _____

If you could easily become "a different person," who would that be?

If you could eliminate a bad habit automatically, which would it be?

WORKSHEET 12

Patterns

What present-life patterns are you currently working with?

Which patterns do you think may be rooted to previous lives?

Are your patterns mostly positive or negative, mostly helpful or stressful?

What are your greatest hopes in life?

When you pray, what do you usually pray for?

If you could do something exceptional for humanity, (not for yourself!) even though it might sound impractical, what would you do?

What else would you do for the world, or for society in general?

What is the legacy you would like to leave for humanity?

WORKSHEET 13
Love Relationships

List *three* of the major love relationships in your life. Write about each one:

1.

2.

3.

What patterns do you notice? If the relationships have ended, *how* did they end? What were the real issues?

What did you gain in each relationship?

What would you have done better?

WORKSHEET 14

List *twenty* things that give meaning to your life:

1. _____   11. _____

2. _____   12. _____

3. _____   13. _____

4. _____   14. _____

5. _____   15. _____

6. _____   16. _____

7. _____   17. _____

8. _____   18. _____

9. _____   19. _____

10. _____   20. _____

Analyze your responses. What themes are found here: nature, relationships, career, spiritual matters, etc.?

WORKSHEET 15

When you work with a past life:

What was the predominant pattern of that life?

What was the major lesson of the life?

What was your mission in life?

How can you apply that information to your current life?

Chapter XIII
Healing the Future

A. Envisioning the Future: Milton H. Erickson

In our work with past memories and present experiences, let us also utilize future potentials and healing progressions. Our lives can be improved and enhanced by our study of the future. Dr. Milton H. Erickson was a pioneer in this important research.

Milton H. Erickson, born in 1901 in Nevada and considered to be the father of modern hypnosis, was a pioneer in the use of hypnosis in alleviating pain and in healing. His pioneering discoveries lay in defining the separate abilities of the conscious and the subconscious minds.

At the age of seventeen, Erickson almost died from polio, and it was at that time that he first developed and used his healing techniques on himself to overcome the effects of that terrible disease. During years of chronic and intense pain, he created and refined relaxation techniques and the use of sense memory and self-hypnosis to cope with his handicaps, as well as to alleviate his pain and to promote healing. With infinite patience and determination he recovered, largely through his own efforts, thus perfecting those techniques that later became the foundation for his work as a hypnotherapist.

Although Erickson employed age-regression in examining a patient's past, his primary focus was fixed on the patient's successful future. Memories were utilized to re-educate or redirect present memories in order to project a positive future outcome. Dr. Erickson broke ground in the use of future progression and future perspective. He encouraged his patients to concentrate on their successful accomplishments, rather than on getting bogged down in past failures and mistakes.

Similarly, Edgar Cayce (acknowledged as the father of holistic healing) believed in minimizing the faults of the past in order to magnify the successes of the present and the potential of the future. The impetus of Erickson's and Cayce's work was to determine what aspects of the past a person might utilize or "apply" in the present to aid in building the foundation for a better future.

Prior to Erickson, psychotherapists controlled the therapeutic process unequivocally. A medical doctor determined all details of medication, behavior modification, and even therapy goals. Dr. Erickson initiated a revolutionary approach by requesting the patient's higher mind to prescribe methods of help and healing. Few people can perform this task consciously; however, on a subconscious level almost everyone can describe emotions and attitudes, and list expectations. Edgar Cayce would agree with this, saying **self is the best help.**

DR. MILTON H. ERICKSON
INSPIRED LEADERSHIP
Artist: Julia Fierman

Healing, Erickson believed, could be self-taught. He insisted that learning is more than cerebral, and we must not allow the intellect to interfere with the better part of our learning. Feeling is the essential factor, he affirmed. Feeling is very meaningful. We feel with our hearts and minds as well as with our sense of touch. We feel the lessons of the past, the hopes for the future, the realities of the present.

In his work with future progression, Erickson first guided the individual into an actually imagined future wherein a goal was successfully accomplished or a disorder seen as healed. The person was then asked to retreat slowly backward from this future perspective and to observe how an objective was achieved or a healing completed, noting the techniques or disciplines employed by the self. Next, suggestions and visualizations were provided to encourage the person to actually *do* those specific things which were indicated by the higher mind, while in trance.

In the *Journal of Clinical and Experimental Hypnosis*, Erickson wrote, "Thus the patient was enabled to achieve a detached, disassociated, objective, and yet subjective view of what he (or she) believed at the moment he (or she) had already accomplished."

Two years previously he had written, that subjects oriented from the present to the actual future, instructed to look back upon proposed hypnotic work as actually accomplished, often, by their 'reminiscence,' can provide the hypnotist with understandings that can lead to much sounder work in deep trance.

He continued by describing a woman who was progressed three months ahead into her future and who gave a "reminiscent" account of her therapy and healing.

Edgar Cayce's readings also are clear on this same point: "...well that there be kept that continued attitude of SEEING the body replenished, rebuilded in a mental, a spiritual, and a material way and manner. This held by the body-consciousness as seeing these things accomplished,..." (Reading 4482-1). Then slowly work backward to discover the healing formula.

Obviously, not everyone is able to perceive an actuated future. The *constructive imagination*, as Cayce called it, varies with each individual; yet, most future-oriented revelations are realistic and conform to the person's present circumstances. Whether interpreted as an actual future or as a therapeutic fantasy, the trance disclosures are in keeping with genuinely attainable goals. Dr. Erickson clearly stated, "There is no running away of the imagination, but a serious appraisal in fantasy form of *reality possibilities* in keeping with their understanding of themselves."

Applications of past, present, and future are valuable tools in the workshop of the mind. Studying the patterns of the past provides clues to determining how a healing may be realized in the future. This work is honed in the present by using insights concerning *how* the healing was accomplished. Suggestions and visualizations given by the therapist may then be used to apply the finishing touches. The practice of this technique becomes easier and easier – even automatic – as the person integrates what has been learned.

B. Seeing Beyond the Present:

B. Seeing Beyond the Present: Previewing Destiny

I have applied Dr. Erickson's techniques and found them to be effective and beneficial. To convey the usefulness of the procedure, I will discuss a session which I recently conducted with a woman who came to me for a past-life regression.

The woman clearly stated that her goal and desire was to learn more about herself and to discover any latent inner talents or abilities which she might utilize more fully. Although she possessed no previous knowledge of her former lives, she felt that she had always been drawn – inexplicably – to the Deep South.

Her past-life regression proceeded well. In fact, she did go immediately to her life in the American south, in which she had matured to find herself the matriarch of a large family. Other than having become somewhat stern and critical during the last years of that embodiment, her life appeared to have been quite fulfilling. Except for a love of horses (which continues in her present life) few personal interests or traits were revealed which seemed to "carry over" into her current life. It was only after returning with her to the present and then moving into her "present-life future" that valuable information was presented.

Prior to this session, she disclosed that she and her family owned acreage in the country and had plans to build a "dream home." As the current real estate market had slowed, the family's present home had not sold yet. This situation resulted in a delay of construction which might have extended itself for years. Still, as we moved into her "future vision," the family was indeed living happily in their beautiful dream home.

So far, all that we had learned seemed to be logical and predictable information. A surprise twist revealed itself as we explored more deeply into her future.

The woman described the new home as a meeting place for a group of people actively conducting some form of spiritual work. Whenever the group met and was engaged in its special activity, a golden light permeated the room. It was the same light which suffused the countenance of the woman now occupying the office recliner. Here, obviously, was a client who required almost no coaching. She possessed ample information to relay, and continued to progress quite easily with little comment from me.

I followed her journey as she proceeded into her future, and even beyond the time of her death. As she viewed her present life from a higher state, I questioned her about her accomplishments during this life: "How did you gain in this life...? How did you lose, or what could you have done better...?"

She explained in full detail that the meetings and the work being done by this spiritual group were the most fulfilling achievements of her life. It was only after the session had ended that she expressed her regret that she was at this time not a part of any such group, nor did she feel qualified even to begin to organize an association of this nature!

Only time will reveal if the dream house will be built and a spiritual group somehow developed. This woman's potential and direction have been revealed to encourage and to inspire her. Whether she will exert the requisite effort and will continue to view this potential in a positive light will determine her final outcome. *Free will* is the most important variable in the geometry of time.

Many people are skeptical of any concept of precognition, or foreseeing of future events. For most of my life I, too, remained quite judicious in speculating about the future. And yet – not long ago – I realized that I had actually fulfilled a vision of my future which I experienced while in high school, as I was first experimenting with self-hypnosis.

Using self-induction, I had guided myself into my future by asking specifically for career direction. My inner vision was both impressive and somewhat incomprehensible. I observed a bookshelf filled with more than a dozen books and I had written, books which dealt with self-hypnosis, past-lives, and other spiritual topics. I also heard (auditorially) that I would author these books – which is interesting, as I seldom receive information in the auditory mode. Almost thirty years later, some of those books have been published, other manuscripts patiently await a publisher, and a few more are incubating in my mind, as yet unwritten.

At that time, even with those articulate words and a clear vision in my possession, I did not believe any of it, even for a moment. It seemed preposterous to think that I would be an author. I had never experienced any desire to write, much less had known anything to write about. English was not my first language; French was. (I am still uncomfortable with the syntax and subtleties of English.) My parents were simple country folk, and a writing career would probably have been the last thing they would have encouraged me to pursue.

Even more of an enigma was the fact that, in my vision, there appeared to be "tiny" books on the shelf, books which did not make any sense because they were too small to be paperbacks and they appeared to be made out of some material other than paper.

The explanation of this puzzling detail may be found in the memories of my earliest experiments with progression. I had begun my past-life research during the early sixties, after having read the book, *The Search for Bridey Murphy*, by Morey Bernstein. Wondering if I could duplicate his experiments, I purchased a reel-to-reel recorder to tape-record my sessions.

Old recorders, such as I used, were quite expensive and very bulky. It would be a few more years before cassette tapes were invented and available. It is a recent revelation to me that the odd "books" on my vision shelf were perhaps not books at all, but cassette tapes. And indeed, I have since produced several self-help and educational tape sets.

Unlike the client at the office, my "future vision" has proven accurate with the passage of time – and the subsequent invention of the cassette tape! Nonetheless, at every stage of this unfolding of events, I did feel that I had exercised free will and that I could have over-ridden or flatly refused to accept this vision of my "destiny."

That everyone has this free will to accept, reject, or to change life's potential is the primary challenge involved in healing with visions of the future.

HENRY'S FUTURE VISION AT ABOUT AGE 15

C. Healing Your Future

After you have completed the worksheets, you will be ready to evaluate your answers. The questions helped you to consider various patterns in your life. There are no right or wrong answers, only insightful answers. Study and evaluate your material. Take your time with this work, as this may be one of the most important projects of your life.

Written words reveal one aspect of your being, but there are other parts that words do not show: your ACTIONS. Actions truly *do* reveal more accurately than words. Often, we use words to hide our actions. It's not weird; it's simply human. The secret is to make your words congruent with your actions, and vice versa.

By listening to your words, observing your patterns, and changing your actions, you will begin to build better habits. Better habits bring health, happiness, and well-being. An important ingredient in this recipe is "detachment." Detachment is letting go and releasing your emotional hold upon things. The patterns that strongly held you will begin slowly to release, to let go. Emotion is good when used correctly, but it is often misused. Often it binds and controls us. Detachment is a *freeing* process. It starts slowly and continues to build, to heal, to free us.

True detachment is not heartlessness, coldness, or aloofness. It is a spiritual state. It is the realization that Earth School teaches us not to react or to become enmeshed in things that are not for our best good, or consistent with our true purpose or ideals. Real detachment frees us from unnecessary activity and allows us to experience more love, joy, fulfillment, and spiritual growth.

The next time that someone or something attempts to involve you with something you don't want or aren't interested in, just say, "No, thank you." Stand aside and say to yourself, "What a wonderful test to see how easily I can detach from that." Smile, walk away, and go DO whatever is *most* important for you. You don't have to save the world – you DO have to learn *your* lessons and enjoy *your* adventures.

Later in this chapter an example will be given of this kind of "positive detachment." Some examples are quite obvious and most people grasp them immediately. Others are nebulous and require some time to comprehend their deeper significance. Study this one carefully, for I saved one of the very best for last!

D. Being Pro-Active

As you continue to study your patterns and to practice forgiveness, you will learn more about detachment. In learning detachment you will somehow move from a reactive way of living to a self-determined one. You won't be a victim of others' actions because you will choose actions more wisely guided by *your* ideals and purposes.

There is a subtle – yet powerful – difference between action and reaction. In most sports, a team goes on the offensive in order to win. A team – or a person – who is always on the defensive can seldom score many points.

In the game of baseball, for example, a person (or a team) can only score when on the offensive – at bat! A person, or a team, cannot score while on the defense – in the field. At best, the players can *try to stop* the offensive team from making too many points.

Only to react is to be doomed to defeat, for you are allowing others to determine your responses. Reaction is merely a response to the actions or agendas of others, and is seldom productive in the long run. Reaction also leads to extremes of defeatism and defensiveness (although it must be said that defeats are more humbling than victories, and can be instructive!)

To act is to build. Well-chosen actions put you in the affirmative position of strength. Those who respond with action usually choose wiser objectives, and such thoughtful action builds balance and wisdom. Only through *acting* – not reacting – does a person truly take the initiative. Action is progressive, positive, and constructive, and it's much more fun!

Plan carefully and take the initiative for your life. If a cynic should tear apart something that you hold sacred, do not react. Rather, *re-commit* yourself to do something positive about it. Write an uplifting, thought-provoking article for your local paper, or give an inspiring talk to a group of individuals who are open-minded and honest.

Cynics perceive almost everything as bad, boring, or meaningless. They search everywhere for faults. They find perverse pleasure in demoralizing others or criticizing their ideas, but they seldom offer practical or realistic solutions. We can find a learning opportunity in their harsh judgments and criticisms. Don't react; learn, instead. Is there some grain of truth in their argument? If so, use that truth to change and to grow, to become a more effective person.

Use what the cynic states and what adversity presents as resources to help you to reach your full potential. Remember, from the most intense struggles may come our greatest strengths. The hardest lessons may also bring the greatest learning, and the greatest rewards.

Throughout the history of humanity, there have always existed cynics who persecuted others. Wise people use the challenges that they present to act, and grow, and thrive. Their secret is wise action, not reaction. Rededicate yourself to your work or your truth. Work carefully to build upon your chosen goals – not to fortify your little ego, but to help to build a better world.

E. Creative Problem-Solving: An Example

In the second month of my senior year, our high school administration decided to impose a new dress code. New regulations demanded that all male students must not wear blue jeans.

The students wondered why such a rule was instigated, for most of the boys wore jeans on a regular basis. Violators of the new dress code were to be expelled. I privately wondered whether the administration – if many of the students came together to form a strong union in protest – actually would expel such a large segment of the school.

Possessing a stubborn and reactionary nature, I immediately began a movement which specifically encouraged students to *wear* their jeans. There was strength to be found in numbers!

Fortunately one of our wisest teachers, Daniel Kelly, suggested a far better plan. Instead of reacting to the ridiculous new restrictions, why not take the OFFENSIVE? Why not do something totally unexpected and dramatic? Why not wear a suit and tie to class!

And so we did. It was a memorable event, and a lesson which I have always remembered. Everyone was amazed – and especially myself. The incident proved to be one of the most valuable experiences in

all my years of schooling, a simple but highly effective
lesson in taking the *offensive* rather than the *defensive*. On the offensive, we had fun; by acting defen-
sively we would have set ourselves up for confrontation and certain disaster.

In retrospect, thirty years later, I realize that the
real question was *not* the blue jeans. Perhaps the
administration simply wanted to flex its muscles, expecting the students to rebel (and suffer) and then to
knuckle-under to bureaucratic pressure. I cannot explain their motivation.

But the fact remains that Dan Kelly presented a
third – and far better – option to the administration's
mandate. To react would have been harmful; the dress
code wasn't worth a battle. To have surrendered to a
meaningless new restriction, on the other hand, would
only have empowered the bureaucracy. The third al-
ternative was perfect. We obeyed the rules, but from
a position of strength – and with the added blessing
of a sense of humor! We were pro-active in the fullest
meaning of the word. We looked good in our suits, we
felt good, and everyone commented upon the appro-
priateness of our action. We had turned the problem
around good-naturedly and with detachment. Everyone gained and no one lost: quietly the dress code was
revoked.

You may also learn from this true story. Don't
become a victim of reaction. Don't give your power
away – unless there is a good reason. Take the creative offensive, be pro-active and more productive. Determine your destiny and live it fully.

You have a wonderful destiny; it is hidden in your
patterns. Learn your patterns, and their origins, and

**STUDENTS GIVE DAN KELLY A GIFT OF
APPRECIATION FOR TEACHING POSITIVE
SOLUTIONS TO CHALLENGING SITUATIONS.**
Photo: High School, 1963

you will discover this destiny. And when you do, live it to the fullest extent possible!

F. Self-Directed Learning

As you learn more about your patterns and how you create your own destiny, you will become a more self-motivated person. A self-directed life brings a constant sense of wonder and adventure. You also will learn the great difference between being a "critical thinker" and a "cynical thinker."

A critical thinker sets out to examine our basic assumptions. He or she is willing to dig deep and find out what needs changing. The critical thinker accepts what does work and changes what doesn't work. First comes study and research, then interchange with others. Evaluations are then followed up by inner processing or guided reflections. Then, and only then, is wise action taken – on any given project.

A cynical thinker often sounds clever – at first. He or she searches only for faults without offering practical or positive solutions. He looks only at the surface of things – the quick-fix or some aspect of his logic which possesses mass appeal. The cynical thinker is often unhappy and repressed. (It is not a scientific revelation, but from years of observation I have noticed that the cynic is often mentally constipated.)

It is best to be a critical thinker. Be critical in your work. Do not take anyone's opinions as fact. Test everything.

I began this work over three decades ago by testing the Bridey Murphy experiment. The author, Mr. Bernstein, was correct: people do have deep memories.

Those memories contain insight, value, and meaning to the individual. Often, they have links or patterns connecting the past to the present, so that the present *is* rooted in the past.

There is great value in understanding those patterns. The following benefits name only a few:

1. *Self-Esteem*
    You have built some positive patterns (habits or recurring themes) that have served you well. They help you to thrive and to excel.

2. *Potentials for Healing*
    You have created some difficult, negative patterns (addictions and/or ruts) that no longer serve you in a healthy manner. Identifying them is the first step toward changing them.

3. *Direction in Life*
    Patterns reveal areas of stagnation. They also signal areas for potential change and betterment.

4. *Continuity of Life*
    Current-life patterns are usually interconnected with past-life issues. You can, by diligent study of your own patterns, perceive the larger picture.

5. *Individuality*
    Patterns reveal the combination of qualities that are you: who you are, what you are about, what you have accomplished, and mistakes that you have made. Patterns honor your uniqueness.

6. *Kindness and Patience*
   Those are qualities which consciously you can commit to patterns. They are helpful in dealing with others who are struggling with the difficult patterns or lessons in their own lives.

7. *Creativity*
   Studying the patterns of your creativity may show you even better ways to work with your positive potential, creating the most wonderful, loving, successful you!

Patterns have a "down side" also, for in denying them – going to the opposite extreme – or in re-running them, we stagnate. Patterns are painful, pleasurable, or neutral. Those that are neutral hold little importance in our feelings; the pleasurable ones are fun; the painful ones hurt!

In *denying* our past we try to avoid responsibility. There is no growth in denial.

In *re-running* a pattern, over and over, we stay stuck in a rut, unwilling to take new paths. There is no accomplishment in re-running.

In *going to opposite extremes* we see-saw at he far edge of responses. We pretend to change and to grow, but there is no balance in extremes.

We gain and grow by honestly studying our patterns. Then we must accept and help to change them. This is done slowly and methodically by some, quickly and dramatically by others.

In embracing our past – its good times and its hard times – we move from the recognition of patterns to their acceptance. Acceptance opens a new road, a

middle pathway to betterment. Some term this level as
"enlightenment." You may call it "healing." I refer to it
as "fun"!

The fruit of all learning is found in behavior. Positive, productive learning brings positive, productive
results. Negative or destructive learning brings negative and destructive behavior. It is that simple. And
yet, because of the gap that lies between what we hold
in mind and thought and its eventual manifestation as
behavior, some individuals fail to perceive that there
is any connection at all. Sometimes this "gap" between
learning and its resultant behavior modification or
pattern changes may extend to days, or weeks, years,
or even a lifetime. This concept may be explained in
simple words: It is hard to harvest fruits or flowers if
you spend your time planting weeds.

G. The Constructive Mind

It has been said, and in countless ways, that like
begets like; for every cause there is an effect; for every effect there is a cause. It is true: the effects, or
circumstances and behaviors in our lives are the sum
total of our past causes. Such causes may be actions,
beliefs, or attitudes.

It would be accurate to say that our present actions, beliefs, and attitudes will help determine our
future circumstances – even our future lives!

Attitudes and beliefs first begin in the MIND.
Over time and experience they build into action, and
then into results. Wisely, it has been said that
when you change your *mind* you change your *life*.
When you build better thoughts you automatically

build a better life!

Some people have had a wide variety of experiences in the earth, but those experiences build wisdom only if one learns through those experiences. So-called "enlightened masters" are simply ordinary souls who have made many mistakes, but have *learned* and *grown* through those mistakes. Strength builds through struggle; wisdom is gained through experience; goals are reached through challenges.

Night bows to the dawn in the same manner that weaknesses evolve into strengths. Hatred melts into forgiveness; harshness softens into kindness; lessons are learned.

H. Networking from the Heart

It is my hope and prayer that this little volume will touch your life in a positive and beneficial way; if not, please write and tell me about it.

When you are finished reading and working with this book, why not write a friendly, personal letter to a Book Review Editor and explain HOW this book helped or inspired you. Then ask the editor to review the book in a magazine. In this way, a review may touch the lives of countless others and perhaps help them with their own spiritual quest. THIS is the important work – it's called OUTREACH!

This is YOUR great opportunity. If you have been helped, now is the time to help others. If you have received benefit, now is the time, and this is the way, to bring benefit to others.

Some mistakenly assume that the important books are automatically reviewed. Sadly, this is not the case. A book must be recommended first and then, hopefully, a reviewer will read it. When people take the initiative and lead, then the leaders happily follow! As the author of this book – compiled with much help from friends – it has been an honor to share this time and information with you. I pray that you will be inspired and encouraged on your journey. I hope that you *will* work with the procedures and worksheets.

As bonus treats, I have carefully hidden some little treasures in this book. They are in the most unusual and unexpected places, but they are there for you to find. Life itself, like this book, is a treasure hunt. Little golden nuggets of wisdom – little pearls of beauty – are carefully placed within the pages for your discovery and enjoyment.

I.   A Beginning, Not an Ending

In many ways, this book is a beginning work-book. In the years ahead, I hope to see many other books continuing this work and study. We touched lightly **upon a few topics**, and many more remain to be explored. Other vital areas of continuing research will be:

Financial patterns
Family patterns
Patterns encompassing all relationships
Love/hate patterns
Patterns typical of groups of people
Career patterns
Spiritual patterns
ETC!

When people talk about "revolutionary solutions" and "miracle cures," they assume that the answer is to contribute large sums of money. Certainly, money can accomplish some things, but others are beyond monetary "solutions."

This book offers practical and proven procedures, winning techniques, and tested programs. It offers help and solutions that bring results. Best of all, the methods are basically free or have a minimal cost, such as the purchase of a blank cassette tape or a notebook. But low-cost investments can bring high-yield returns. The secret, or the "miracle," is in the *doing*. Through application comes the comprehension and the wisdom. The keys to a spiritual life are not to be found in institutions, religions, governments, or "the media." True and honest answers are alive in the compassionate heart and the enlightened mind of each individual – IN YOU! In the quietness of spirit resides ALL light, ALL love, and ALL that is called GOD.

Chapter XIV

Perfection

A. Seize the Day! Seize the Lifetime!

L ife is a great and powerful adventure. You are already LIVING that adventure. It's not a theory: it's real, it's here, it's now. The fullest expression of that adventure is in reaching out and helping others - in *serving* others! It starts by getting your life in working order; then you can reach out to help and to encourage others.

You *already* have taken the first steps in the bravest and boldest adventure of all time - the journey into your heart's memory. Keep your heart's purpose straight. Keep your eternal vision clear.

You have dug deeply into your memory. Sometimes, to get to the root of things, you have to dig in the dirt. You may get your hands dirty - but it washes off! You may weep, but the tears wash and cleanse the soul. Your efforts will be rewarded.

Some people — especially children — *like* to dig in the dirt, they love to touch the earth. It's important to learn lessons, but it is equally important to have fun also. Let your inner child come out and play often.

Theorists may tell you that the purpose of life is to reach perfection. That may be true, but *what* is perfection? Is not perfection living life fully and truthfully? Is not perfection just living a simple and kindly life? Is not perfection living your daily adventure?

Remember to take time, to make time for retreats and reflections. Wandering in the wilderness you can re-think the purpose of your life. You can re-discover the hidden treasures of the heart. You can re-connect with your higher mind through the mystic cord of memory.

Growth occurs in resolving problems, happiness in living life productively and in loving others. Everything you do reveals what you are - so study and learn the lessons. Heal the difficult patterns of your past. The only bad lessons or patterns are those in which you fail to learn.

Be especially kind to young people, they are the hope of the future. They are the bridge to *your* future. Teach them to be kind. Encourage them to be generous. Nurture spiritual values. Share with them the secret of eternal life.

We learn through doing, and in doing we live what we are learning. Earth is the adventure! I pray that you will graduate with high honors from the University of Eternity.

B. A Poem

Perfection

I want you to be perfect.
You want me to be perfect.
I want me to be perfect.
You want you to be perfect.

We want them to be perfect.
They want us to be perfect.

And no one meets the criteria.

So, we criticize and call it constructive...
    we gossip and call it news...
    we generalize and call it Truth...
    we throw away people and call it progress...
All the while struggling to protect our own fragile
    essence.

When will we learn
    to be ourselves?
    to trust each other?
    to embrace the lost and lonely?
    to celebrate this moment?

Because
All we really have is each other
    Today.

-Rosemarie Jacky Deering

Please direct all correspondence to:
Adventures Into Time Publishers
P.O. Box 88
Independence, Virginia 24348 U.S.A.

"Power Tools" for Personal Improvement
Books and Tapes by Henry Leo Bolduc

*Self-Hypnosis: Creating Your Own Destiny
Now in its 9th printing, contains 31 scripts and full instructions for making your own self-help tapes. Self-hypnosis is a valuable tool for healthy living. Receive your recommended daily allowance of positive programming and creative visualization.
Quality paperback, 190 pages $9.95

*The Journey Within
True accounts of the author's experience in guiding regressions and helping others to channel their higher minds. A fascinating journey into our deepest memories.
Quality paperback, 299 pages $12.95

*The Journey Within - Cassette Tape Series
Eight valuable guided sessions for spiritual growth and betterment: Cassette 1: Ideals/Centering, Cassette 2: Spiritual Opening/Eternal Self, Cassette 3: Past Life Exploration/Hall of Records, Cassette 4: Exploring Between Lives/Vision Quest. Eight sessions, instructions included, 4-tape set $35.00

*Healing the Past — Building the Future
Cassette Tape $9.98
Side 1: "Discovering the Healer Within." Everyone has healing potential; everyone has healing gifts. This session will help you to acknowledge your healing gifts and will help you to heal the healer within.

Side 2: "Your Extraordinary Journey Through Time" is our newest session for age-regression, past-life exploration, and future progression. Progression is the history of your future!

*Embracing Your Eternal Child
Cassette Tape. $9.98
Side 1: "Embracing Your Eternal Child" is a session to help you to connect with that innocent and wonderful child within, to experience the incredible healing power of love. You are guided to your inner sage or mentor.

Side 2: "Inspired Writing or Drawing." This exercise helps you to write messages from your Healer-in-Residence, your Financial Advisor, your Inner Jester and your Higher Self. You also can ask for your Soul's Name and its meaning.

*Life Patterns, Soul Lessons, and Forgiveness
Quality paperback, illustrated $14.95

Order Form

Adventures Into Time
P.O. Box 88
Independence, Virginia 24348

Name _____

Address _____

City _____

State _____ Zip _____

Payment by check or money order, payable to Adventures Into Time, P.O. Box 88, Independence, VA 24348. Please, no phone orders. Money Back quarantee if not satisfied within 90 days of purchase.

QTY	TITLE	PRICE/EA	TOTAL
		SUBTOTAL	
VIRGINIA RESIDENTS ADD 4.5% SALES TAX			
		SHIPPING AND HANDLING	$1.75
		TOTAL